Gene Daly

12/25/16

I Met Marilyn

By

Neil Sean

FOX
NEWS
LIVE
BETWEEN ATTYS FOR SAN DIEGO MAYOR BOB FILN   NAS   3,622.89

Written / Produced / arranged – Neil Sean

A Maycon Production

C Neil Sean 2016

All photographs c Maycon Productions / Neil Sean / Mark Grant

Assisted by the following snappers / recorders and cameraman over the years who include

Sharaz Ali, Justin Downing, Daniel Mason, Jim Seldon, Harry Brandwatch, Michael Dias, Luca Roveri, Hector Sole, Daniel Howard, Edward Asta, Asha Basia, Spencer Marks

Neil Sean would like to thank personally, Ann Montini, Mark Grant, L B Mayer, Daryl Zanuck company, Rupert Murdoch, Fox Films, Fox News, NBC news, CBS news and the many other organizations he is affiliated with

Elements of this book were written in the following hotels

Hilton Hotel – New York

Hilton Hotel – Blackpool

Marriot Hotel – Bournemouth

Millennium Broadway Hotel New York

Much grateful thanks to all for assisting in accommodation and hospitality

Maycon Publishing

Part of the Maycon Entertainment group

So much has been written about the life of Marilyn Monroe, since her untimely death in 1962. Fired by her studio 20th Century Fox for not completing her last film "Something's, got to Give" and tragically passing away at an all too young age of just 36.

But as I reveal throughout this book be prepared for another story about the Marilyn. It's fascinating what I have been able to build up over the years through my role as a TV presenter, Journalist, and broadcaster., What I mean by that is simply everyone I have worked with who ever encountered the great actress has such a brilliant story to tell and as such it's a totally different account from the many previous books as simply they are telling me about the Marilyn they knew, met with and laughed on the phone too. From such greats as the wonderful comedian Sir Norman Wisdom, Respected director Billy Wilder who worked with Marilyn on two of her most famous films through to Dean Martin's son Ricci who has a young boy, met Marilyn towards the end of her oh so short life and gave a totally different perceptive on tragic last stories we have heard about so many times

So why write a book about Marilyn Monroe after all there are so many already what can you add that no one else has? That was the response that came to me from many people when I began this project and true what could I offer but as you will see what I found out was nothing short of amazing about her, and I think even if you're not a fan you will be at least given a different view of her life to date,

Marilyn Monroe has touched so many lives with her acting and persona plus her great beauty having met and interviewed so many stars in relation to her they all agreed that she would be stunned to think that at this stage in world events and time she would even be remembered but as she famously said herself "I just want to be wonderful "

The Final days.

Marilyn Monroe awoke very early that final Saturday morning. She had slept very badly. She looked at herself in the mirror long and hard and for a long time, she had told friends she dreaded waking up as there was always a new line or facial mole to deal with and it just confirmed to her that she was ageing and fast. Although thinner than she had been in years, she looked tired. Despite those special Liz Arden electric facials, she needed a manicure and a pedicure. But first, feeling the lonely start of another long and very empty day, she needed to talk. But who should or could she call? One of her ex-husbands? Her psychiatrist? The White House? Even old fans who she had befriended from time to time during her lonely moments and radio call in jocks?

As with all Hollywood legends, the last day of Marilyn Monroe's life is a mystery. The 36-year-old actress spent Saturday 4 August 1962 at her Los Angeles home. By early next day she would be dead, found nude by her housekeeper, face down on her bed, clutching a telephone receiver, an empty bottle of Nembutal capsules at her side. When news of her apparent suicide broke the next day, America was astonished that the star had been without a date on Saturday night, but she told a close pal "I never expect a date now I mean why would I? Here I am the most famous women in the world yet all alone on a Saturday night. why is that? It was a question she would often ask yet never got a response simply because there was not any answer that could quell her desire to be loved and wanted. it seemed she had her pills. they would never let her down

So was it suicide or murder? Was Marilyn driven to despair by the recent end of her love affair with President Kennedy? Only a couple of months earlier she had sung "Happy Birthday, Mr President" at Madison Square Garden to great acclaim, but he dumped the relationship cruelly soon after. Had she embarked on a new relationship with his brother Robert F Kennedy? Marilyn was known to keep a little black book documenting all her affairs and conversations. At the time of her death, Hollywood rumours were circulating that she was about to announce a press conference the following Monday, while this is true this was more to reinstate herself as a commodity, actress, she had agreed a new deal with her studio FOX who had fired her two months previously. While others speculate about what she had planned Tony Curtis told me "she wanted basically to get back out there and let the world know she was back and raring to go. Marilyn I knew was having affairs, but truly this was her wanting to feel needed and viable. her been thirty-six and a sex symbol was more of a problem

The coroner's official verdict was "probable suicide". Marilyn was represented as a professionally unreliable, pill-popping depressive. Nervous - she suffered many things including rashes, hysteria, sickness and other illnesses which could be triggered by tension or arguments – Many of her critics argued she had simply gone head first into self-destruction. Terrified of abandonment she feared turning into her mother, who had spent most of her life in a psychiatric clinic.

The previous year she was suffering from a dark depression, Marilyn had been checked into the Payne Whitney psychiatric clinic. To her shock, she was locked in a padded cell. It was only when she phoned her ex-husband, baseball star Joe DiMaggio, that she was released she never quite got over that experience at all

That fateful last August day, Marilyn, her critics sniped, was an aging Hollywood sex symbol with a career that was finished. Pale, thin and lifeless, her hair was ruined by bleach, yet she never wanted to use wigs "I have to be real "she insisted she wouldn't leave the house without her make-up man and hairdresser to prepare her as she too felt that if the public saw her looking "real "they would all agree it was over for her such was a paranoia. She had been cruelly fired by Fox and replaced on her last film, Something's Got to Give yet even the replacement failed to take off so the studio which claimed she had cost and lost them $2m in delays rehired her. Her love life was a mess, with the end of her marriage to the playwright Arthur Miller. She was embarrassingly at a low point in her life so who would be that surprised if she had decided to end it all?

The many people I interviewed insist that Monroe had never been happier. Moving from New York to Los Angeles represented a fresh new start. She had bought her first ever house and was refurbishing it which she liked to call "Mexican Modern "Yes, she was self-

medicating too much and receiving psychoanalysis to cope with the end of her marriage, but in the week before her death, her career was very much back on track, in fact, better that ever. She was the cover star of both Life and Paris-Match. After seeing the triumphant and ground breaking nude rushes of Something's Got to Give, Fox had rehired her - she was due to report for work again on Monday. Her previous 23 movies had grossed more than $250m.

Every year, it seems, a new piece of the news emerges. Way back in 2004, of tapes that Monroe made for her psychiatrist Dr Ralph Greenson, appeared she gave to him the day she died, were published, revealing her to be far from suicidal, in fact, she never sounded happier Then a letter written by Monroe to her method acting teacher, Lee Strasberg, was made public for the first time appeared. Although composed eight months before she died, it shows Marilyn's plan to set up an independent film production company with Marlon Brando and how who they were going to work with ... Not really someone who was ready to end it all do we all agree?

On that final day and night Marilyn's agent and self-proclaimed "best friend, Pat Newcomb, stayed over on Friday. She says that the actress woke up feeling groggy through obvious lack of sleep, but was very excited about a delivery of furniture from Mexico which she has bought on a recent trip there in the previous February. Her housekeeper, Eunice Murray, arrived at 8.30am, she claimed Marilyn was already up, tiling the floor and singing while doing it.

Newcomb woke up at noon, and she and Marilyn argued, apparently when Newcomb's ability to sleep put her in an instant bad mood, it was soon resolved. Pat then says they planned to sunbathe by Marilyn's s pool, then maybe join the actor Peter Lawford and his wife Pat (a Kennedy sister) for supper. She has since added that Marilyn was not that keen on the idea as she seemed to have "fallen out with Peter over some issue "

During Saturday morning, Marilyn's mood dramatically changed. She was very annoyed and stunned by the arrival of a stuffed toy in the post with no note, she felt uneasy about its arrival but according to Pat Newcomb did not "wish to discuss this, many phone calls ensued. Murray, the housekeeper, has stated that Marilyn asking a rather odd question of if they kept oxygen in the house, Had Marilyn already begun to fear for her life? aware that she was a political liability. "John F Kennedy was going to run for a second term, Jackie had to be happy with all of it. They needed Marilyn out of the picture". That was the general Conesus by many who knew of the situation at that time according to many of her friend's I have interviewed

Pat Newcomb then decided to go out shopping and said Marilyn was upbeat when she returned. But her psychiatrist tells of a rather different story so was Marilyn who had a duel personality hiding something from Pat? Dr Ralph Greenson, who had arrived for his daily visit, states Marilyn was in a highly emotional condition, weeping, laughing and then banging her fists on the wall. a totally different story now emerges.

Greenson asked Newcomb to go home which she did with no quibble. again an odd move, and then asked Murray to stay overnight with Marilyn.

The doctor left according to his statement at 7pm. Marilyn took the phone into her bedroom and Murray claims she never saw her alive again. Lawford says he rang Monroe at 7.30pm and she sounded depressed and slurred. He claims she said, "Say goodbye to the President and say goodbye to yourself, because you're a nice guy", before her voice faded out. However, his view is dismissed by Joe DiMaggio Jnr, the son of her second husband, who says he phoned her at 7.30pm to tell her he was breaking off an engagement she disapproved of. He says Marilyn was in a very good mood at the news. In fact, she went to speak with the housekeeper Mrs Murray who was busy watching an episode of Perry Mason on the TV to say how delighted she was at such news

Later that evening, Marilyn was found dead. Murray woke up and claims she saw a light under the door, again a rather strange situation as the doors were hard to close due to the extra thick carpets that Marilyn had recently fitted and has been proven since you could not see any light underneath. Worried that something terrible had happened, she called Greenson at 3.30am. They peered into Monroe's bedroom window and saw her naked body. Greenson says he broke in with a poker, before ringing Marilyn's physician, Dr Hyman Engelberg, but the window had been mended by the time the police arrived. Something that no one could claim why it had been mended and at such speed

While these details have been challenged over the years, and it is undoubtedly true that Murray was an unreliable witness but more of that later. That August, Monroe had fired her she felt she was not a great housekeeper even stating that "I have to buy the food and the cleaning supplies so what is she doing exactly? Her last contracted day of work was Saturday 4 August 1962.   In 1985, after years of denying it, Murray admitted during a BBC interview that Robert Kennedy had visited Marilyn's s home that day; a claim backed up in 1993 by Murray's brother-in-law who worked as Monroe's handyman. Murray also let slip that an ambulance had arrived while Monroe was still alive. Yet why did she only reveal this information near her own death?

So No one really knows exactly how many people had access to the house the night Marilyn's body was found. So many papers were destroyed, telephone records seized. Were they searching for that little black book or in fact the press release she had teased Kennedy with earlier in the day?

Sydney Guilaroff, her hairdresser, says Monroe called him twice, quite hysterical, to say that Kennedy had been at her house with Lawford threatening her. The last phone call Monroe made was to the White House. Was she calling JFK? There are even rumours that she spoke to his wife, Jackie.

So ended the life of the most famous woman in the world. As Monroe's body was wheeled out of the house it passed over a tile embedded in the entrance of the home with the Latin inscription,

Cursum perficio, which translates as "I have run the course" - or "My journey ends here". It seems unlikely the journey will ever end.

Meeting George Cukor

George Cukor was one of Hollywood's most successful and versatile filmmakers: a master of the musical drama, the comedy, the domestic thriller, and the literary adaptation--not to mention a great director of actresses, including the likes of Greta Garbo, Katharine Hepburn, Joan Crawford, and Judy Garland to career-defining performances. I was lucky enough to meet him as a young boy with my trusty tape recorder while he was staying at the famous Savoy Hotel in London and filming "The Bluebird "with Elizabeth Taylor and sometime pop star Patsy Kensit, He agreed to meet with me I believe simply because I had written to him directly and explained that I was a fan of his work and quoted many of his films to him. Remember this is long before the internet so you had to be a fan to

know such stuff and he was impressed I knew that. George or Mr Cukor as I had been told to call him by his assistant was not what you would call that friendly and years later seeing the uncut footage of him directing Marilyn in "Something's Got to Give "you can see how this was the case. He warmed to me eventually but listening to those faded C60 cassettes now make me realize how fortunate I was to land such an interview ... Mr Cukor was well into his seventies at this point I might add but always dressed like he was attending a premiere. Jacket, expensive shirt cravat he looked and smelled divine. I think he liked me because I was dressed in a smart suit with a bow tie so he could see I had made the effort too. Our meeting took place in the main afternoon tea area to begin with but because of the noise of the other people he suggested we went to deluxe suite which was at the top of the building ....

Once seated with tea and cakes, he simply said fire away. we talked about so many starts and studios from Louis B Mayer at MGM through to Daryl Zanuck at Fox, and so we began our chat about the world's most famous blonde Marilyn

He told me the movie "Something's Got to Give was Initially called Goodbye Charlie, the film was a remake of My Favorite Wife. The picture, Marilyn's last under her Fox pact, was approved by production head, Peter G. Levathes. Hoping to get the film made without interruptions, for which Marilyn was notorious, Levathes met all of her demands. First, Marilyn demanded that they let go producer David Brown as "she just did not like him really I think more so because he was not that much of a fan, to begin with and she sensed that she knew who tapped into her she was bright for sure".

Then, the script had to be rewritten, costing the studio an additional $125,000 dollars. Again George states "she was very clever you know because she knew what played well and she kept telling me that " Marilyn would not do this or she would not do that so again she should have had far more control that she was credited for simply because they were her original ideas " She was upset with director Frank Tashlin, so Fox brought in me at a cost of 250,000 dollars I liked her so had no problem, we knew each other well and had made " Let's Make Love " a few years previously so I knew what I was getting into you know I knew her quirks quite well and what bothered her the most " . She also insisted on hiring her hair stylist Sydney Guilaroff and Jean Louis as costume designer. Finally, the studio also accepted her choice of Dean Martin as leading man. But that was because as George puts it "Rock Hudson has turned it down, so had Paul Newman and quite a few others. It was because you know Marilyn was a long term commitment and they were not that keen on all of that work. I know she liked Dean a lot but he was not her original choice, I think she felt he was too laid back and not big enough at the box office along with her ... George added "She felt and I know this that she was losing it a bit and figured if she shored it up with a big screen man then it might just work

In this version, Marilyn plays a lost aviatrix, a married woman, and mother of two kids, who comes back to her husband (Dean Martin), who in the meantime has attached himself to another woman (Cyd

Charisse). A new facet of Marilyn was revealed in her scenes with the two children. Wanting, but unable, to have children, Marilyn's relationship with the kids was lovely. She was genuinely interested in kids, delightfully rolling on the floor and playing with them. George reveals "That was the only part in the film I felt she was totally relaxed because they did not judge her you know she just showed up looked nice and was really sweet with the young kids so no pressure that and the nude scene which was her biggest moment".

Shooting was to start in November 1961 but was delayed to April 1962. On May 5th, the film was eight days behind schedule, and Fox had already invested a million and a half dollars. At first, Marilyn would call in sick at 6 am, but then the calls stopped and she simply didn't show up. "We can't afford her and Cleopatra too", was Fox's reaction; Liz Taylor's absences boosted the cost of Cleopatra to over thirty million. Monroe's absentee record showed just five performance days out of seven weeks of shooting. The picture was 32 days behind schedule, costing more than 2 million dollars. Of her five days, only two were really good. Dean Martin, who was at first undisturbed by Marilyn's absences, told the press he was "the highest-paid golfer in history".

George then relates that A replica of my house was built on the Fox lot, including his noted swimming pool "The reason for this was that I knew what shots we could take and how we could take them plus I had invited Marilyn over a few times to the house to get the feel of the set. You had to do things like that to secure her really"

In the episode, Marilyn was trying to woo her ex-husband by exposing her charms in a brief skinny-dip sequence. Cukor first asked Marilyn to do it in a flesh-coloured bikini, but the subterfuge was so transparent that Cukor conned her into doing it for real. A year ago, she was 15 pounds' overweight, and would not do it. But she has trimmed down and was back to her great 37-22-35 measures. When Cukor suggested to do the swimming pool scene nude, she agreed without a murmur and looked exquisite in it.

George's take on this was rather more direct "she looked good for sure, but the face was too thin now she looked severe in some shots, and while still stunning without a doubt she was no longer the young women she was so the body was the way forward you know. show it off and then hopefully it became a talking point " George also pointed out that she cried a few days into the shoot when we brought in those big reflector screens because she knew that they were brought in to make the face look younger she had seen it with other actresses on set and told me "I know this is the beginning of the end of my sex symbol days I know what happens now "George also confided that he used a new style "Obie spot" light which basically blasted a sharp ray of light directly onto the face removing all lines "I did what tricks we had back then I mean I used soft focus anything because I knew she cared about her looks far more than anything else on the movie".

The nude scene got a lot of publicity, with stories about Marilyn going back to where she came from, before gaining respect as an actress. George though explains "she needed a hit, and she looked good. we had moved into the sixties and people were already doing some weird things in movies so to be the first to do a nude scene was well again something she could enjoy and celebrate "Plus he added "you see Neil there were no lines to learn just her and the water so again very easy to do plus she looked great and wanted to show us how she looked to prove she was worth the wait and all the trouble she gave us "Tight security gripped Fox's Stage 14 that day. The set was cleared of hangers-on, and electricians were asked to look away. Clutching the pool's grim, Marilyn was more bashful about showing off her stroke than her figure. "All I can do is dog-paddle", she told George. "That will be just fine, darling", said the director. But again George adds "I think she was a good swimmer actually but by doing the paddle it meant she could keep her head above water and show more. her face and that dazzling smile. we all felt we had something good on camera and so figured this was worth the wait and she knew it I knew it we all felt that day we were finally on track "George at this point got a bit teary

George told me he was irritated and amused by Marilyn's acting coach and companion, Paula Strasberg. Her immortal line, "My Lee (Strasberg) says, 'it's what's on the screen that counts.'" That's what she would say when Marilyn would appear for a few hours once in three weeks. To me, George recalled Paula Strasberg was pretentious, ridiculous, and not very nice. She was a freeloader her and that husband totally free loading of people who had talent. Not many knew that both were really failed actors, yet they were "teaching "and I use the term loosely others to act. I blame her for many of Marilyn's problems I really do she was a sweet girl without much guile that was her basic problem

The company had been assembled in April, but out of 32 working days, there were only 7 and a half usable minutes of film. Almost a million dollar over budget, shooting was postponed several times because of Marilyn's various illnesses. When Marilyn did show up, late, as usual, she was nervous about being late. George would reassure Marilyn by telling her not to worry or be nervous because she was worth waiting for.

When Marilyn was out, Cukor filled it in with cover shots of Martin and Cyd Charisse, who played the second female lead. But they ran out of material–Dean Martin reacted to the script girl and anybody else they could find. Cukor was furious, when suddenly one noon Marilyn scampered off the set to a helicopter, flew to International Airport at Inglewood for a jet to New York. This was on a Thursday, two days before the President's Birthday party at Madison Square Garden, on May 21. Defying the studio's edict not to go to New York for the President's Ball, her trip through an entire crew of 104 people out of work for half a day on Thursday and all day on Friday. Monroe insisted the studio had been notified months in advance she was going to the party; the studio denied ever permitting it. The studio was even more annoyed, when Marilyn did not show on set on Monday, June 4, after making a personal appearance at the Dodgers Game, on Friday night, June 1st.

George though viewed these things rather differently on my tapes because as he put it "What a coo for the film now looking back. here is our star singing for the President of the United states I mean we should have been paying her really but again this was a different time. I knew though she was on thin ice I knew it, but she was

buoyed up by her friendship with the Kennedy's ... they were
powerful, and she felt by association that she was then too. I think
looking back the whole film was doomed as she did not believe in the
film and neither did Dean so with me thrown into the mix It was
shall we say going through the motions of what it could have been
and should have been".

After three weeks of work, she came in for 2 days then flew off to
Washington. For Cukor, it took the nerve to do that She went to the
baseball game Friday night and couldn't come to work on Monday.
And there was certain ruthlessness, 104 people show up every day
and go home. Hired by the day, the workmen come in in the morning
and sit around. "Here are these men", Cukor told Hopper, "and I
hate to sound patronizing, but they are married and have children,
and they have to sit and see this money thrown away. George tells
me he thought the studio should have replaced Marilyn weeks ago,
but it was run by people who had no experience, it really was I mean
Zancuk was out of it filming somewhere in Europe and the young
bucks they had hired really had no idea on how to make a film they
should say to me., "If we can get her in for just one day". "What
about the other days", I said.

In the end, George resented "Marilyn's problems, her plotting,
bullying and outsmarting the studio, making outrageous demands,
and the studio stupidly giving in on every point". I did if I am honest
because it would have been wiser to pay her off and finish up her
contract without her doing another film for them, but back then
studios worked differently and so it went on".

The studio issued a formal announcement of star's dismissal, explaining that Monroe's removal was necessary because of her "repeated wilful breaches of her contract". No justification was given by Monroe for her failure to report for work many times Suffering major losses through these absences, Fox took legal action against Monroe, filing a $750,000 lawsuit against her. Lee Remick was seriously considered as a replacement, but Martin did not think she was right for the part, though he had the greatest respect for her talents. "I signed to do the picture with Miss Monroe" Martin said, "and will do it with no one else".

George though told me "The whole Lee Remick plot was pure PR she basically was around and under contract plus she fitted the costumes and this was basically dirty tricks on Fox's part to make Marilyn sit up and point out to her that no one was unreplaceable. They knew this would hurt her but let's be honest no one could replace her, and she knew that too".

George also gave me an insight into the world of Marilyn at that time because she said "she loved attention and wanted to know who was dating who but she would never ever consider herself to ask a man out. she was Monroe you know almost Cleopatra and thus men came to her so When Sinatra got engaged, Marilyn went mad, knocking her head against the wall. Getting closer to her, George realized there was no sane procedure to her; she had obsessions, one of them was refusing to pursue a man and more importantly that she was the sex symbol and wanted to hang onto that for as long as she could but again she knew it was slipping out of her grasp age wise.

"Marilyn was very sweet with me" added George, but he felt enormously sorry for her. "Marilyn has these people around who disliked her really.

Charlton Heston

Charlton Heston was one of the most dedicated and talented actors of our time. His movies are regarded as some of the most epic and successful in history. Two of his pictures, 'The Ten Commandments' (1956) and 'Ben-Hur' (1959), are among the all-time top-grossing films. I met Charlton Heston quite by chance one day in 1985 when he appeared in London at the Queen's Theatre in 'The Caine Mutiny Court Martial'.

It was one of those moments that you cannot plan simply because I was new to London and was basically looking around. The Queen's theatre stage door is in the heart of Soho which back in the 80's was a bustling vibrant place and ideal for someone who was looking for fun and excitement of the big city. I had noted the stage door and I was really just looking at it as I do with all stage doors when a voice came up behind me and said "Excuse me"; I turned around and there standing right in front of me was a well-tailored man with a great smile and very tall with a Stetson hat on. It was Ben Hur no less Mr Charlton Heston, it was around 2pm and he was gearing up for a matinee performance of his new London Hit Play

I must point out at this time I was doing all kinds of jobs to survive so while I had begun writing shorts stories for magazines and pieces about living in the city I was nowhere near doing what I am doing now. My look was to be kind "New Romantic" as I was also hosting a night at The Hippodrome Night Club and also starting out on my stand up career so the weirder you looked back then was a bonus so I could see why Mr Heston was well looking at me with rather dubious eyes.

I turned around and said "Mr Heston I know you don't know me but thank you for giving me some great viewing hours on film. I suppose you get this a lot but I am a huge fan of your work "He smiled and said "Thank you that is so kind of you".

As he worked his way into the stage door, I asked him if it were possible to get a picture with him as I had been advised many years earlier to make sure you secure a picture so that whatever happens people will know you actually met them. "Sure" he said and turned around, now this was the problem, I did not have a camera. You see, back in the good old day's people did not just hang around taking selfie and snapping everything that came into sight so you had to have a camera. I told him "Mr Heston, I don't have it on me right now but can I call back later as your one of my favourite movie stars" he looked at me and said "No problem, just come back to the stage door in between shows, I would be delighted to pose for a picture with you". I was struck at how kind he was and sincere but again he was a studio product and knew the value of real fans.

He went into the theatre and I dashed off to Boots to buy one of those newly disposable cameras that were all the rage and basically the only one I could afford at that time. Looking back the problem with the cameras was that you had to rely on someone else taking the picture and of course you did not have a view finder so you had no idea what you or the victim you had taken looked like and more importantly if in fact it had turned out alright.

At the duly appointed hour I returned to the stage door with new camera in hand only to be met with sour faced stage door lady who knew that I had been there previously but chose to ignore that fact and told me "If you don't have an appointment then I can't let you in". I noted that there was a number on her wall which I memorized and decided that fighting her was a waste of time. I went outside and rang the number of which she answered and in my best US accent asked to be put through to Mr Charlton Heston's dressing room, it worked and once again I was speaking directly to the great man himself ... I had to be quick as the pips on the payphone would start but I explained my dilemma and he assured me I would have no further problems in getting in to see him.

Sure enough I was whisked through to the dressing room which was rather dark and dingy but then all dressing rooms are. We quickly posed for the picture which I was not sure had taken and then we *began to chat... Charlton seemed to enjoy having a young fan who knew all about Hollywood and his career and we spoke at various lengths on his successes and failures.*

When I brought up Marilyn he was genuinely sad he told me that they had finally seen each other at The Golden Globe Awards in March 1962, "She looked stunning and I mean stunning because we had not seen her for some time in public. I would say she was a bit of recluse really so when she did appear all heads turned and she was there to pick up an awards which I along with Rock Hudson and Stephanie Powers presented her with".

Charlton or Chuck as he told me to call him went on about how she was at that event, "She turned up with his guy (Jose) and he was a real user, you know, the type that knows been pictured with someone will do him so much good but Marilyn, I think liked the fact he paid her a lot of attention but he was far younger than her and this was a problem because he had an eye for the ladies and not just Marilyn. Let me tell you, the thing is by the time she came up for the award she was steaming drunk, I mean, steaming drunk and uttered just a few words and departed off the stage leaving us all a bit loss of words ... It was the sort of stunt she may have done at the start of her career but now she was really playing up the dumb blonde role and was well not well behaved". Chuck added "So were back stage and she lunges for me and starts to kiss me all over thanking me again and again for the award but I tried to tell her it was nothing to do with me". He noted "Marilyn was very lonely and felt she had no friends there really. She was not happy with Rock Hudson because he had turned her down to be her co-star in her latest film

'Something's Got to Give' so she was a bit sore with him and then after the event, she rang me to ask me if I would like a cameo in her next movie. It came as a shock because at that time she had very little idea about the movie or its plotline".

As we sat in his dressing room it was not hard to see what Marilyn found attractive about this man, back in his prime he was one of the biggest stars in Hollywood so it would make sense that she would want him to be in the movie to add box office "Marilyn you know, a lot has been written about her but I felt it was a tragic end after what she told me. We were sat chatting and she kept placing her hand on my thigh and giving me the come on look when I told her "Look Marilyn you're a swell girl and I think your beautiful" she stopped me right there and added "But you don't want me do you?" I had to gently explain that I was happily married and while it was flattering that she was looking at me I did feel that she did this as a way of total control because the room was filled with some of the best looking men in Hollywood at that time so why me? Was it because I was not showing interest in her. It always baffled me really but I did wish I could have helped her".

Charlton finished with "I never saw her again after that, as she departed the awards she was virtually carried out with her team of people and the guy but she looked so unhappy and thanked me for my kindness. I did get calls from her from time to time but I never knew how serious they were as she told me she wanted to work with me but I knew this could be dangerous". Charlton also revealed that it was not just Marilyn who was all over him "Rock Hudson was a nice guy but could not respect the fact that I was not that way inclined, he kept asking me very direct questions and if I would like to meet up secretly all that kind of talk. When I brushed him off he talked about my body and roles in the movies. He was a pretty full on guy really. I liked him and here is the thing you know Marilyn refused to believe that Rock liked men, she asked me about the stories and when I confirmed that she looked stunned and said "Are you sure? because he always looks at me the way man looks at a woman, you know", so I don't think she kind of got it the whole gay thing and I am sure she would have been stunned to find that she became a gay icon, you know the biggest in the world really. Charlton was great fun and as our time came to an end he offered me tickets to the show he did ask me though not to repeat our conversation until way into the future as "Its delicate you know I don't want to upset anyone and I would hate for anyone to be offended by me". Charlton also cleared up the story of 'Let's Make Love', the 1960 movie for Marilyn "I never turned down the lead role as I was not offered it as such. I had not seen a script and the only thing I knew about it was that it was a Monroe film so that story is not correct. I would have loved to have worked with Marilyn as I felt she was a good actress and the potential to be an even greater one but I know that story does the round"

I saw Charlton again via various TV stints and promotions and as I was climbing up the ladder of the TV world, he was always polite and kind in interviews at events like Oscars and Red Carpets. Oh the picture well yes you guessed it I took it to Boots in Piccadilly and because there were only three snaps on the camera the girl thought there was something wrong with the film and. exposed the footage so all I received was another free camera and a black roll of film ... but I did get some wonderful audio tapes and memories.

<u>*Sir Norman Wisdom*</u>

The London-born star was known for his slapstick film roles in the 1950s and 1960s, famously playing Norman Pitkin against frustrated boss Mr Grimsdale. I became good friends with the comedy legend through my parents and Norman even came to my hometown of Mirfield to help launch his own range of VHS comedies at our local library. However, Norman could be a huge handful as he knew how to get an audience but he also loved to tell a story and his friendship and meeting with Marilyn was the stuff of legend. Marilyn was of course at Pinewood in July 1956 to film 'The Prince and the Showgirl' with Laurence Oliver. Now not many people may know that Larry as he was known as a great fan of Norman and even

admitted to me how he studied him while making 'The Entertainer'
film when she starred as a failed music hall comic Archie Rice.
Norman told me "I liked him too because he cared about his craft
and he knew what he wanted; I think the stories of him and Marilyn
not getting on were true, well he told me they were but I think the
real problem was that she made things look easy even though he did
not and that stuffed him really because he thought he could be the
big shot when in fact she stole the film off him to be fair".

Norman told me he was aware of Marilyn on the Pinewood lot while
he filmed 'Up in the World'. "She came in to watch my work. In fact,
she quite unintentionally ruined a couple of takes. Marilyn could not
help laughing, and on two occasions she was politely escorted off the
set. The nicest thing that happened was that we passed each other in
the hallway one lunchtime. It was crowded, but she still caught hold
of me, kissed and hugged me, and walked away laughing. Everybody
in the hall could not believe it. We had a few cups of tea and she
came to my dressing room for a chat, she was a great girl and not at
all depressed like the people paint her out to be. I think the bigger
story was that while she loved been a movie star she also wanted a
family and I think she was more fascinated with my little children
Nicolas and Jackie, she really wanted to know all about them and if
they were going to go into show business too. I would always talk to
her about them as I think it made her happy, she giggled when I told
her the daft things they did". Norman though says that part of the
problem, as he saw it, was the fact that Marilyn had a stern boss in
Larry Oliver and then another boss at home with Marilyn's new
husband Arthur Miller. Norman been Norman he was blunt and
revealed "He never cracked a smile and always looked like

everything was beneath him, you know, and always ready to dash off like he was way more important that what we were talking about"; Norman added "I got the feeling he was not happy at how she could create something by just been well, you know Marilyn so he always wanted to deflect away from her, she was good she always directed things back to him and tried to make him feel part of things but to me he was a misery guts and I never warmed to him". Norman said that he loved his time with Marilyn and he pointed out a little known fact that "In the 60s when the Carry On movies were getting huge the producers spoke to me about Marilyn appearing in their spoof 'Carry-on Cleo' which was a huge send-up of Fox films big screen version starring Liz Taylor "Fox had left all their unused sets on the Pinewood lot so they made the movie with the left over sets but they really wanted to secure Marilyn in the part and wrote to Daryl Zanuck who owned the studio" Norman laughed and admitted "they never heard back funny enough but can you imagine what she would have been like and how much fun she would have brought to the role…"

Jack Cardiff

Jack Cardiff, the cinematographer, was a master of the Technicolor process and created the intoxicating, highly brilliant atmosphere of the Powell and Pressburger films 'Black Narcissus' (1947) and 'The Red Shoes' (1948). He worked on the 'Prince and the Showgirl' with Marilyn in 1956 and was one of her biggest fans.

I met Jack Cardiff quite by fluke to be honest. At this time I was working in regional television and this accounted to me appearing on regional chat shows like 'Lunchtime Live' which had various guises across the daytime ITV network in the late nineties, I had been booked to appear on the Meridian TV version of the show and as per had no idea who the guest were going to be so when I arrived at the studios which were based in Newbury in Berkshire, I was still unaware; when I was sat in the green room with this very kindly elderly man who was very chatty. When I asked him what he was on the show for, he said to speak about his career as working in films.

Can you imagine my shock when he said what films he had worked on? I learned a lesson that day and sharpish because you can always assume that they may not be something but everyone has a story and everyone is special. I found that out while we chatted naturally about working with Marilyn on the 'Prince and the Show Girl'. Jack revealed "At the time the film was shot in London, Oliver, 50, was at the top of his profession, having been knighted and having starred in and directed acclaimed adaptions of Hamlet and Richard III". Jack told me that Oliver regarded Monroe, at only 31, who had starred in mega hits like 'Gentlemen Prefer Blondes' and 'The Seven Year Itch', as his inferior. "Olivier went out of his way to be a "pain in the arse" to the American, deliberately seeking to antagonise her by "unwisely" allowing his wife Vivien Leigh, the star of 'Gone With The Wind' who had played the part of the showgirl on stage, to attend the shoot 'Now Jack' added "Marilyn was in awe of Vivian and felt sorry for her because it was touted around and by Larry that while she had played the role on stage she was simply too old for the film version so while Ms Leigh was kind she was also seething on the inside as you can imagine watching this younger stunning blonde piece openly making love to her husband on camera...It was a scene and a half".

Larry's obvious hatred of his co-star seems largely to have been based on her refusal to socialise with the cast and crew, and her obsession with method acting, which led her to question every decision he made as the film's director. But Jack also pointed out that it was also to do with the fact that she was more famous and that was something with his ego he found hard to take "He was even at that stage of his career, known as the king of the acting world, I mean he often told you he was not that shy in self-promotion when you look at it".

Jack went on "she took no heed in any of that as many famous people don't she took it in her stride but I noted that both Larry and Arthur Miller were in parts annoyed at the instant attention she received when she went out or simply appeared anywhere really".

Marilyn resented his treatment of her and was particularly hurt by his refusal to acknowledge even her status as a sex symbol, she knew though that she had blown her chance to become under her spell as she told me "I think he liked me while we met in New York, I mean, I could tell he liked me and I know a lot about men but then he did not want me as well he saw me as a rival and threat so again quite difficult to manage when you're an actress who is supposed to be in love with your co-star".

Jack told me he was sympathetic to a point with t Olivier, who died, aged 82, in 1989, he remains loyal to Monroe. Jacked painted an image of Marilyn as a sex symbol who had an almost child-like quality off screen "she did this wide open stare thing on camera but in a way that was her you know she was in awe to many things I mean look at her. Life in a very short period she took over the world, she created Marilyn Monroe which was some achievement in many ways".

Jack also pointed out that Marilyn's punctuality and inability to turn up anywhere on time was not arrogance, but shyness. "She really was gripped with shyness and would often tell me that she was not ready yet to "summon her up quite yet". By that she meant Marilyn the character she had created so without that she was you know left to her own devices which meant crippling shyness and something she had to overcome a lot of".

Jack remembers with fondness a trip to the theatre could be enough to create a panic attack: "When we got inside, we were sitting in the stalls about 10 rows back and everyone sitting in front was just turned around looking at Marilyn. During the interval, to stop us being mobbed they had fixed up a little private room for us. The first bell to signal the end of the interval went, and we got ready to go, but Marilyn asked for another drink. Then the second bell went and she still wouldn't go. I looked at her and she was obviously terrified of going back. It was that bad but while I could read it Miller, the husband could not or simply could not be bothered so he yanked her back into the theatre and well marched her back in".

Jack told me of his last meeting with Marilyn, just months before her death, gave him a revealing account into her private hell she was going through. He remembered: "I went over and it was a big room with just one dim light like something out of an old movie and she was wearing dark glasses. She looked terrible in many ways because she had lost a lot of weight and while it looked great on screen she looked visibly older and more drawn plus she seemed to be in some kind of fog. It was hard to get through almost like she was in a trance with herself". We sat together and had a drink and she told me what a terrible time she had been having.

"She told me that she went to a health farm and that in the end it was some kind of asylum. She noticed that the door handles were missing

on the inside and she couldn't get out. She had been told that she could only leave if a relative came and took her, but she had no relatives by this time. Joe DiMaggio, her second husband, who was a wonderful guy and who always stood by her, came and got her out". Jack added "she had a terrible fear of madness and going mad so the person who did this really knew what buttons they were pushing with this treatment and it worked she was a total wreck". We spoke about our time in England and she asked me all about Oliver and if he had ever forgiven her? "I pointed out I think he has nothing to forgive and he should be thankful, you agreed to star in the picture". She thanked me for been so kind and asked again what she should do next she spoke softly". I think you know you had a good understanding of me and what I can offer as an actress. I do want to act but I know I do rely on my attributes way too much she giggled".

Jack also remembers that she was acutely aware of the shifting times as they had reached the early 60s and that she knew her type of character was on the way out hence the slimming diet "I have been on a high protein diet of liver and eggs I wanted to look good again and show people I can change my look and maybe play other roles? "she did look great but again in the flesh sat opposite her now with dark glasses, roots showing and a hap hazard clothing arrangement you would never have known that this was the world's biggest sex symbol. That was her beauty though she could switch it on or off and you could be stood right next to her and not realize this was Marilyn but then she could create it right before your eyes it was a one off magic" recalled Jack.

Jack told me that he truly believes that the actress, who was credited with committed suicide in 1962, was in fact murdered because of her brief affair with President Kennedy. He is convinced that a reported sighting of Robert Kennedy at the star's Hollywood bungalow is crucial to the final end in her story. "She was not the type for sure. I know she appeared down and often fed up with life but she also knew her worth and what she wanted to achieve out of it so no I never believed that she killed herself. An accident with pills maybe but again she was surrounded with all kinds of shifty characters", Jack continued "she alluded to an affair with very important people high end and was almost begging me to ask who they were but I knew that she was like a teenager looking for approval and why or how could I approve of that".

"She also told me that she was looking at maybe taking time out from her acting work as she may have something bigger to occupy her time which got me thinking she honestly thought she may have ended up marrying one of the Kennedy's but I pointed that if her new man was catholic and well that high up he would have to take some pretty big knocks to do so".

As we sat there chatting about things I noted that if this was the case and she was so happy with his new man why was she sat all alone and no one to be with, after all we had been working partners a few years back but not great pals so I knew that she was in another world of her own really which left me quite sad. Jack told me the final thing she showed him were sketches of costumes for the film 'Something's Got to Give' which were designed by Jean Louis, "I think they look great don't you? "she asked liked a child willing you to like them so that all could be all right with the world", Jack added "We kissed each other goodbye and that was really the last I saw of her but I think she would have got a kick out of people still to this day talking about her and buying her films. She really had no idea just how much she would become so loved".

Sandra Howard

Sandra Howard (nee Paul) was one of the leading fashion models of the 1960s, appearing on the cover of American Vogue two months running. She worked as a freelance journalist alongside modelling, before turning to novel writing. She continues to write regularly for the press. She is married to the former British Conservative Party Leader Michael Howard.

It's funny how you meet people quite by chance who have an association with Marilyn and quite out of the blue, I was aware of

Sandra Howard after all this elegant former model had graced TV screens and stood beside her husband Michael on TV so you got the impression that this was something of a catch but I had no idea she had mixed in such circles and this fascinated me. She had a book to promote and I thought she would make the perfect guest on the chat show we have, so we invited Sandra along, a naturally shy and nervous person on camera. She had a wealth of stories about her time as a model and, of course, how she met and chatted with the legend that is Marilyn along with Frank Sinatra too. What I wanted to know having seen the pictures was, just how easy was it for a model back then to be pictured with two of the biggest icons in the world.

When you look back she told me it "it all seems quite surreal. I was just 21 — rather shy, with a stammer, but I was also a successful model with Lucy Clayton's agency in London. It was a different time then because models today are household names but back then people knew you but unlike today it was not a profession like that you know it was fun something you did before you got married as it were". Sandra added "I was married at the time to Robin Douglas-Home, and because Robin's family was aristocratic and well-connected — his uncle, Sir Alec Douglas-Home, was Prime Minister in 1963-64 — we also had an entrée into the world of America's political elite yet it was not on with me as it were I just sailed along and took it all for granted .We had my first child Sholto whom Frank Sinatra became his godfather and he was thrilled when we asked him, that is how I ended up meeting the Hollywood sex symbol Marilyn you see – Sandra had been invited to Bel Air to a party at Sinatra's home and she points out that Frank was a darling, a total

professional and far more caring about others than people gave him
credit for Sandra's husband, Robin. At Frank's invitation had
agreed to give Robin unprecedented access for a book he was
writing about his music. We were to be Frank's guests for three
exciting weeks and it was just like been in a Hollywood movie with
all the A-list stars around like Peter Lawford who was dashing,
Dean Martin, Sammy Davis Jr you name it they were there but it was
a serious business writing a book about Frank's music as even then
he was well an icon". Sandra agrees that "she enjoyed the high life
that mixing with the heady cocktails of these people at that time was
superb but also I also remember with affection the times spent in
quiet domesticity at Sinatra's Beverly Hills home. He was the perfect
host and you know really looked after you that is where I met the
glamorous Marilyn Monroe". Sandra continued that "I loved her of
course through her movies and figured that all men must fall
instantly in love with her and I do believe at that period of time that
Marilyn and Frank were in fact an item. He thought so anyway".
On one occasion he invited Marilyn Monroe to supper: we ate,
without ceremony, on little trays as though in front of the TV.
Marilyn was a delight. Shy and warm-hearted, she spoke in her
trademark self-deprecating semi-whisper. I warmed to her instantly.
She was wearing white Capri pants and looked stunning, I mean
stunning and a bright orange sweater cut tight to do full justice to
her gravity-defying bosom. Which had every man in the room
looking at her yet she almost seemed oblivious to that fact. Either
that or she was simply a better actress than people had her down
for; Frank told us both discreetly that she needed cheering up but
didn't tell us why. They appeared affectionate and together which
got me thinking that Hollywood stars are all the same really, we all

fall in love and it does not matter who with. I really wanted to speak with her but as I say I was terribly shy myself and I also thought what does a twenty-one-year-old model say to a worldwide movie icon other than "Hello". Her memory stays with me forever though as she had the most powerful presence and like everyone I was shocked that she was taken so early. I doubt she had any idea what an icon she would become but at least I can say I met her".

Sandra concluded our chat with the news that she too had looked at acting for a career option even back in the early 60s Sandra recalls "It was my first ever trip to LA, the legendary producer David O. Selznick had offered me a screen test which was in itself terrifying to be honest as he was a giant in cinema. Sadly, for me though my stammer — and the shyness that was all connected —and it did not quite work out as planned, or my career might have taken an entirely different course of direction but I really have no regrets at all".

Phil Silvers

Jewish comedian Phil Silvers, also known as "The King of Chutzpah, " was a popular comedian of the 1950s. Silvers started his career on stage in vaudeville as a boy singer. He made his film debut in 1940 with Hit Parade of 1941 and went on to act in a number of films. He is best known as the fast-talking gambler Sergeant Bilko in The Phil Silvers Show, a 1950's sitcom set on a U.S. Army post. He co-starred with Marilyn in her final film "Something's Got to Give".

I met Phil or Mr Silvers as you had to address him when just a mere child but as I have stated before I was lucky enough to meet with him while Dad was busy with the BBC. I knew of him of course because his show "Bilko" was huge on our TV screens back then and I loved his wise-cracking persona which was new and refreshing plus I had seen him by this age in the famous Carry On film which he proudly told me he was the "highest paid ever actor to appear in one of those films "I am not sure the bosses whom I met actually thought he was worth it to be honest. I met Phil as I say but I was a little in awe of him as he talked fast and really had no time for anyone but himself and he let you know it. There was not a sense of reality with him but I did like him because he spoke a language I truly understood showbiz and above all else he told me that he was the best...in his price range.

We spoke of his time on the film with Marilyn and he told me how he actually got the role "As ever in Hollywood they needed laughs and I knew that while Dean Martin was a great guy it as Jerry who was the comic so the studio bosses at Fox decided that I would come along and play some business with Dean on the film as a show point you know some gags back and forth which we did mostly adlib really. "Phil went on "There was of course Wally Cox too but I knew why they had hired me and we got on well really but Marilyn was someone else I mean totally something else "Phil pointed out that Marilyn looked great and she knew it and how he was there on the day she filmed the infamous nude scene in the movie".

We got the message that she would be filming this scene which created havoc in the studio I mean you would have thought that these men would never have seen a naked woman before but after all this was Monroe and well we were all getting a little excited".

Phil went onto to say that George Cukor seemed happy on that day as she "knew she did not have any lines as such to say so figured this may work out quite an easy shoot".

When Marilyn appeared the set was sealed off basically but we knew the spots to view from and while I am sure she wanted to create a sense of privacy this was Marilyn so she knew the rumpus she had created on the set. She looked sensational though I mean she had a women's figure not a girl but because of her new image she looked the best I had ever seen".

Phil continued that while he liked the director George Cukor "well this was a first rate movie you know and this was a big deal for me, it had huge stars and a good potential I was playing an insurance salesman called Johnson in the movie which was fun and not too demanding, when suddenly the whole project was up in the air".

"Because of the way Marilyn was and I mean this kindly she was difficult I mean we all knew of her involvement with the Kennedy's because she talked about it. Sure it was in hushed tones but this was a big deal back then you know a movie star and the President but what always bothered me was why she thought she would be any different from the other broads I mean she was Marilyn Monroe but I knew that Kennedy was not a keeper he had a lot of ladies on the side so while we all heard we knew it could not last but it appears that Marilyn believed it could.

Phil also went onto to say that "she was not a bad actress at all but again I blamed this whole damn method thing she did because we are making a comedy and yet she is looking for meaning I mean it's a comedy just play it but honestly by this time she is so wrapped up in it all she could not see the light, Phil added "The thing is she was great her own ideas were spot on and if you see the rushes she could almost direct herself yet she had no belief so if someone made a change to the script it threw her yet her suggestions were knocked back yet she was the star for goodness sake.

Phil concluded " I do think at that time she was focused her career as such she was as we all knew secretly heavily invested in The Kennedy's but even she must have known how much they used people I mean she was a lovely girl but as much as I liked the family I knew that she was not bound to be included in their world yet she seemed to think so " Phil added " I think she would have been stunned and happy to see how much she is remembered because she was not sure about herself at all and her status as a movie star is beyond words I think she would have been really happy about that

Eartha Kitt

Singer and actress Eartha Kitt is best known for her holiday song "Santa Baby", and for playing Cat woman in the 1960's TV show Batman. It's funny when you meet people along the way with a Marilyn Monroe connection because while I knew of her as an artiste I was stunned to discover her story and her thoughts and memories of the blonde icon.

Eartha Kitt came into my life simply because at that time I was working in the record industry and loved it. We're talking mid-

eighties here and the sound of Eurobeat was huge. Eartha had recorded this great track "Where is My Man "which appeared on her 1984 album I Love Men. The song was co-written by comedy writer Bruce Vilanch along with musicians and producers Fred Zarr and Jacques Morali. Where Is My Man" reached the Top 40 on the UK Singles Chart, where it peaked at number 36 This was her first UK Hit single in 28 years, the previous chart entry, "Under The Bridges of Paris" dating from 1955. The single was also a hit in dance clubs around the world peaking at number 5 in Sweden and number 22 in Netherlands. In the US, the song made the Top 10 Eartha was back on top and raring to go, this is how I met her also my father had some dealings with her as she appeared in the world famous Batley Variety Club in the sixties and so when I got introduced I used this connection and she spoke fondly of him and her time in Yorkshire where she told me "You have the best markets in the world truly so good value "and gave that famous purr of hers. Eartha who was knocking on at this time but still looked great and carried on in that old showbiz way that real stars do was appearing in a club night in London's Charing Cross area. The Club was a tad notorious to say the least and when I arrived backstage to have a chat I was struck at how she must have felt playing such a place having given concerts in the leading halls of the world but she would have none of it she told me "Darling it's showbiz and I am having a ball, I am back in the charts again and enjoying life embrace it all " She was getting ready for the show which was a late night affair where she would mime to a backing track while simply being this glittering legend on stage and while she got ready we spoke of Marilyn " We were both lonely and used by men to an extent but I don't want you to feel sorry for her because she did not... I remember speaking with her while she was in the throes of getting rid of the playwright and you know the thing is she blamed herself and not him. Can you imagine that she laughed "Eartha stated that Marilyn helped her career a great deal "she was vastly ahead of her time in terms of race relations and just acceptance of people really I mean if she liked you she liked you and that was it".

Eartha though did add "I don't buy the fact that Marilyn was anything but dumb at all, I mean she took on her own studio which was big back then you know a women like her stating she wanted to run her own production company and all that I mean really but she did it to great success but you know she knew she had brains and beauty and that is one powerful thing when you look at it". Eartha said that she was not surprised to hear of her sad demise: "I was so upset because she could have reached out but the thing is she always wanted you happy first she was totally selfless in that way... I remember one receiving one of her old fur coats to wear at a premiere because she heard me saying I did not have one. What a kind gesture and again to someone just starting out in the business amazing lady and one I would never forget".

I met Eartha quite a few times after that she was a gracious lady and highly talented like Marilyn we won't see her like again in such a hurry...

Bette Davis

The darling that is Bette I met on quite a few occasions due to the fact I hung around the studios at BBC TV centre while she appeared on Wogan which was a huge chat show back in the day and while I was working away bringing guests into the show for Terry he kindly would introduce me to people that he knew I would like and of course Bette was wonderful and nothing like her character at all but also a tad terrifying at times without doubt.

Bette appeared with Marilyn in the classic "All about Eve" which focusses on ambitious actress Eve Harrington worming her way into the lives of Broadway star Margo Channing, playwright Lloyd Richards and director Bill Sampson. This classic story of ambition and betrayal has become part of so many cultures. Bette Davis claims to have based her character on the persona of film actress Tallulah Bankhead. Davis' line "Fasten your seatbelts, it's going to be a bumpy night" is legendary, I hear that that Ms Bankhead was not keen to hear this as she too had for a time been in line for the role "but, in fact, all of the film's dialog sparkles with equal brilliance Marilyn played with great comic effect Miss Casswell.

Bette was kind and generous with her time on the many occasions I met her and was the only major star who was not too bothered about my trusty tape recorder Bette told me in between huge puffs of smoke back stage at the Empire Shepherds Bush" Marilyn Monroe, who was just starting out in pictures when she made All About Eve was very insecure working among such great established talent and struggled to hold her own. I know along with some of the other actors could get impatient with her inexperience but she tried and tried hard and I told myself this girl is doing her best". Bette cackled "I know this does not make a great story but I can be kind and you know she was wonderful in the role I mean she looked great and *people were telling me she was going to be this next big thing but I don't recall thinking that myself she seemed lonely to be honest even at that stage of her career".*

Bette also let me into a secret about her co-star George Sanders who she claimed "was hot for blondes and he liked Marilyn a lot after all he was ambitious and of course she was on the rise but Monroe's presence caused the most trouble for co-star George Sanders, who plays Addison De Witt. Sanders was newly married to Zsa Zsa Gabor at the time, and Gabor was none too pleased to have her husband away on location with the breathy blonde bombshell Bette laughed again "I liked Zsa Zsa but she was no actress more of a celebrity if you like so for her to Knock Marilyn was kind of odd".

Bette told me that the thing that impressed her about Marilyn at this period was her ability to work when she finally got to the studio " She had created this character and it was in development but she knew that this was the one that would get her the most success and so it's hard to come up with that character every day and I knew it she knew it so in many ways we bonded " She told me all about my earlier films but not in a fun way but in a way that she had studied them and that was very impressive because they Cleary had stuck in her mind and that again played to my flattery.

Bette though could be kind and she told me "we had some scene together and she was so nervous she came to the set shaking and told me she had hardly slept the night before and what did I do for nerves and so forth. Anyway we rolled the cameras and she kept blowing her lines. It had to be done in ten takes in the end because she kept on doing this. I knew that the whole crew were wondering when I was going to explode but I did not "Breathing out yet more smoke she told me "I just felt bad because I knew this was terrible for her inside and I am willing her to get it right so when she did we had a hug and she gave me such a lovely smile. A little later during the day she came by to say goodbye and thanked me again and said " I just hope the lines stay in but you never know " I told her she was magical and that it would be in the movie and of course it was " Bette though gave some rare insight into the Marilyn at that time " she would arrive at the studio without any makeup or hair and smeared in Vaseline on the face which baffled me as she was very young but already had a preoccupation about ageing " Bette went on " We discussed this once and she told me many of her tricks to keep age at bay including having a satin pillow so that it did not create lines on her face at night and many others now which escape me".

Bette continued "I told her a great actress should not be worried about lines of ageing because this can help with her character and part but while she agreed she came in every day with the face full of Vaseline so again you did wonder if you were ever getting through to her I know the director of the movie was kind and patient with her but to a point you know.

Bette though also threw light on Johnny Hyde and is involvement "He was in love with her but not she him yet she was kind and gentle with him and they got on well I would say he knew the score but in way I do wonder if he had lived where it would have gone as she had no intention of marrying him she told me that she said "He is a great *guy and I do love him but I want to marry for love and that is not something I feel about Johnny".*

Meeting Bette Davis on every occasion was hard work to say the least purely because she was a god's gift to any interview and she fired off so many things about legends but she finished on this with Marilyn "I was not stunned to hear about her death I mean they say Hollywood killed her but you know I believe that she could not live up to the hype she had created, the myth and all that. I do believe she felt she had not created enough work to feel happy as yet but she was getting there. It was all so sad. A brilliant girl really".

Joan Rivers

Joan Rivers, the raspy loudmouth who targeted on the world's obsessions with flab, face-lifts, body hair and other blemishes of neurotic life, including her own, in five decades of great comedy that propelled her from nightclubs to television to international stardom, Joan was to me a great star and when she told me of meeting another one. You can imagine how excited I was. Joan was a great lady and very kind actually, I have her to thank for introducing me to Prince Charles and over our many chats at various suites in London hotels like The Ritz, Savoy and so forth you got the sense that like our other icon once the applause stopped she was lonely. Joan had done many things in her career but she told me that the star of her career she ended up at a dinner party while she appeared in a

terrible off-Broadway show at which she met Marilyn. This was
towards the end of her life so Joan told me it was around early 62

"I was stupid you know because I had no idea how I ended up at this
party but it was great none the less and quite a few big names there
but because it was New York good people just talked business,
theatre and I had landed the invite because of appearing in a
Broadway play. Marilyn was sat on my right and she seemed very at
ease in the situation but what I remember most is how tiny she was
you know just tiny thing not the big buxom blonde we see and hear
about all the time in the media". Joan continued so the dinner is
being served and I foolishly introduce myself and say I am an
actress".

Joan told me that you must take the story as it stands at that time
because while Marilyn was world famous she was not an icon then if
anything this was just prior to "Somethings got to give "she looked
great and was very modern but no icon if anything she was hoping
as they say in the world of showbiz to make a "comeback".

Joan continued "We made small talk about New York theatre and
what my plans were and then I asked her about acting agents, she
was really helpful and because Lee Strasberg was there and a few
others like Arthur Miller, Elia Kazan and Lee Strasberg that Marilyn
Monroe turned to me and only just 17 and in my first year at
university – and said: "Men, they are all the same. They are just
stupid and they like big boobs". Joan added she was stunned
because the conversation was not going that way but she just said it
and I loved her for it because you know she knew what it was all

about for her boobs and nothing else so again you wonder if she was far brighter than anyone ever thought because you know I did".

Joan went on full flow " She looked stunning but kept referring to these liver spots on her hands and saying you know like Madonna does now how she would have to wear gloves because they would say she was getting old and all that stuff so way ahead of her time " Joan told me that she felt Marilyn was murdered " without a doubt I mean sure she was a pill addict and had problems but also none of her final story stacks up I mean given all she had going for her why would she suddenly kills herself and also she was not the type you know .. Not the type I have met many people who are. Like anyone who goes to a Yoko Ono concert all look like they are ready to do it" she laughed " Joan became serious for a moment and told me " I think looking back I am glad I was not around in that time because Marilyn told me what she had to do to get famous and you know it got me thinking that after all that she then was worried about a few liver spots " Typically Joan she made a joke about certain elements of the Kennedy's and stated " You can see why she fell for them because they had the charm, the looks and power .. At dinner that night she spoke of opening her own theatre and putting on plays. I think she was passionate about acting in many ways but at that time there was no way a studio would back her "Finally on Marilyn she added "I do wonder if she would have lived if she had married someone normal you know, the thing with Marilyn was also she was not a great gay fan. No sir she loved them but loathed that all men could not find her attractive I told her about my gap pals at University and she looked bemused by it all. I mean she had a hard time believing Rock Hudson was gay because she told me "I am not sure about that "Well proved what gander she had then

Joan admitted that looking back she could not quite believe her luck but again stated "You're young and starting out to me Marilyn at thirty-six seemed a woman you know what I mean not like me a young girl so I am in awe of her to this day and yes I blame the Kennedy's without a doubt she got mixed up in some terrible trouble really".

Jack Lemmon

Jack Lemmon was one of the most popular film comedians of the 1950s and 1960s, widening and deepening his reputation in later life with a number of acclaimed dramatic roles.
He was the first actor to graduate from winning an Oscar in a supporting role - in Mister Roberts (1955) - to winning a second in a leading role - for Save the Tiger (1973). He became known as many did as a Marilyn costar in the quite rightly epic "Some Like It Hot".

As I have stated previously this role I landed enabled me to meet so many of my idols and Jack was one of them simply because of "Hot "I really loved the way he played his role and the scene with the Castanets on the bed could cheer anyone up no matter what they are ailing. I met Jack when he was starring on The London stage at the Theatre Royal Haymarket in Long Day's Journey into Night, which was a huge success and he was so thrilled that it was. That is what I remember about him really he was over the moon with the box office and gave me a guided tour of the theatre which was and remains *wonderful and at this point I had no idea just how much that theatre would play in my own career.*

Jack though loved to chat and our first meeting took place in the stalls of the theatre where we got to speaking about "Hot "and how he landed the role in the famous movie but before we got started he told me "My favourite pastimes are golf, pool and the piano, so as you can see the movies did not figure into that for me. I love acting I really do but it's not life and death for me. Money to eat and live now that is what is important at this stage of your life".

On Marilyn he told me quite directly I used to live at Harold Lloyd's old house— and one day I was coming back to the house and there's this helicopter in a low lazy circle and these guys in funny suits and funny glasses standing around watching Marilyn Monroe and JFK having a frolic in the pool So whatever stories you heard about Marilyn that one is true for sure she was in a deep relationship with JFK now if he thought the same we will never know but she was not at all embarrassed by what I had seen and remember I had seen quite a lot of Marilyn from the movie so just to clear up all the stories yes for me there was and it was a big affair for her " .

Did you know that jerry Lewis was also offered the role of the zany "Daphne?" Jerry turned it down because he "didn't think drag was funny So when the movie comes out and is a huge hit and all that I could not believe it so I used to send Jerry chocolates annually in gratitude I mean he would have been great in the role but I am not sure according to Billy Wilder anyhow how much she and Jerry would have got along together because he is a genius and all that but also creates things adlib which Marilyn was not great with. Jerry later admitted he regretted his rejection of the role but as Jack continued "I did not need to have the story explained to me as Tony and I were thrilled to be working with the brilliant Billy Wilder I mean who worries about the story with that calibre on board".

Jack went on "Frank Sinatra was another early choice to play my role "Daphne" but I thought if he changes his mind I knew that Marilyn really liked the idea and she was pushing him and pushing him because she thought they would be good box office plus of course he was great with her on sets and things. Anyhow Frank says no thanks and Billy again was secretly casting around so it was not a given that I was going to get the role you know although Billy told me it was mine there was talk around town that Rock Hudson was been lined up too so quite difficult really".

I have to mention that at this point a very young actor came over and started to chat to Jack without any look in my direction and then kind of hung around. His name Kevin Spacey, While I thought he was rude again I was mistaken as he was just simply very shy and basically now looking back as older and wiser figuring out who I was, was I useful and if so why was I not interviewing him. We have met many times since then and he always remembers it as I told him "I am so sorry I forgot your name". He thought this was so funny as did Jack because it took the sting out of his tail and he knew that I knew he was not impressing me when you have Jack Lemmon in front of you.

So Jack goes back to Marilyn and says "I really liked her very much and we both got along great with her. She had a lot of problems by that I mean a lot of problems yet no one seemed to know what they were. I will say this though now looking back at what she created which in effect was Marilyn Monroe must have been hard to conjure up day after day on a movie set but Billy Wilder was a nice guy and he had worked with her before so he knew what she was going through in parts.

Jack elaborated "she was a very unhappy girl as I say why? Who knows but I am sure she knew that she drove Billy and Tony Curtis nut and yes, she drove me a crazy too but I didn't let on and it didn't bother me as much as it bothered them, without a doubt it was almost always the same thing: the lateness. She had a problem, with ever getting anywhere on time but again age is a wonderful thing and now you can see just what she went through I mean I liked Arthur Miller but I had no idea what they had in common he was always a terrible misery on set and always wanted to rush hear way as if someone may just point out what a bore he was you know".

She simply just could not come out of her dressing room, fully made-up and dressed and everything it was like a force field at the door and then people had to persuade her and all that plus I felt for her makeup man because she would always find fault with her look on the set and claim it was the makeup or she looked too fat etc., Jack added " she was fat though at that stage because she was expecting but none of us knew and she loathed the way she looked on camera but all I see is one sexy girl in her prime again she saw things totally differently "Anyway She just could not and would not come out. Now and then, you heard stories that she was drinking a bit but again I never saw any real evidence on that myself but rumours go around on sets. I know the extras loved her because they got paid overtime and they openly loved it when she failed to show up on time. Quite a few got new things like cars and paid off homes on the back on the lateness we all went through, , But when you look at her performances she was wonderful truly great and I mean she steals every scene she is in so again was she right to make us all wait until she got that " magic moment " Jack also was not a great fan of Marilyn's acting coach Paula Strasberg " You do ask the question what use was she but I loved the way that Billy Wilder got shot of her with his classic put downs and all that he was superb at getting his own way ... We would hear Paula tells Marilyn "Now in this scene think of a meadow full of golden flowers and channel that "What bull when you're making a comedy but this was a job and in a way maybe Marilyn needed her. I always felt that Arthur Miller thought she was a crackpot but because she was the breadwinner and not him I figured it was what she said made it work and even if he did not like her well what could he do. He was on the Marilyn payroll too really.

Jack was in a playful mood when he asked me "Did you know Mitzi Gaynor was the original choice for the female lead "Sugar Kane" role, but as soon as Billy found out Marilyn Monroe was available, he offered her the role. I am sure Mitzi was fine about it but again can you imagine anyone but Marilyn now in that role and you can't really can you?

Jack admitted that like so many he was not shocked when he heard of her passing. "We were due a meeting actually because Billy had an idea of a film and we both said well Marilyn would be great in this, Of course the movie became "Irma la Deuce".

Marilyn liked the idea and we had chatted about it, I had seen her a few times over the last few months and yes she looked great well in fact totally different in many respects but she was slimmer and had different hairstyles when we met, I think she was trying to recreate and move ahead with the times so again she knew what she was doing and this final images are some of her strongest yet when you look at them " I had heard reports about her last movie and all the stuff that we had gone through but I did think it would be worth it as look at what we got with her so when the ending came it was sad but genuinely I just hoped that she had found the happiness she was looking for really ... " Jack added "she had a lone force around her and let me explain this to you. Marilyn was friendly, fun and well vibrant on many occasions but there was something about her that said "Keep away that is far enough for me".

Jack continued "I think for sure she should not have gotten mixed up in the clan that she did but again she was the type of girl that looked straight into trouble and no one could ever advise her so the ending I suppose was partly her destiny..."

Jack left me with one line that he figured I would find amusing he told me that "Did you know on its original release, Some Like It Hot was banned in the state of Kansas. Cross-dressing was considered "too disturbing for Kansas. When I told Marilyn this she laughed and laughed because you know she had all the best costumes so I think she felt she was next to me and Tony the world's number one sex symbol and here was the proof".

Jane Russell

Jane Russell, was among the most desired women of the 20th century. She had great erotic force and great comedy skills. Russell only made just over 20 films, but only a handful of those are remembered: her first film, The Outlaw (1943); the comedy western The Paleface (1948), with Bob Hope; and the musical Gentlemen Prefer Blondes (1953), co-starring Marilyn Monroe.

I met Jane on quite a few occasions. The "Wogan" show, plugging her book and various things like her Bra line which was genius when you think about it and maybe something Marilyn could have done had she lived that long, my father had also worked with Jane as oddly enough in "lean "periods she had agreed to come over to the UK and appear in WMC clubs which Jayne Mansfield had made a career out of in her later years.

Jane though was a force of nature and always defended the Marilyn myth and spoke with kindness and grace about her famous co-star telling me "She just needed to know you liked her and you know at that time Fox thought we were going to fall out when we were doing Blondes but we got along just swell and remained friends until her death".

Although Jane and Marilyn made Gentlemen Prefer Blondes together - and were well-matched, particularly during their duet, Two Little Girls from Little Rock - their ultimate fates turned out to be dramatically different. As Jane told me "I was a simple girl and really had no desire for fame as such, it came to me but in a way that kept me ground and I felt good about it because I was not living for the next movie and Despite their differences, she warmed to Marilyn.

Jane told me "You see Marilyn's first husband, Jim, went to high school with me so we had that connection and .one day he came by and said: 'I want you to meet my wife'".
It was Marilyn. "She was very a pretty girl I mean not the Marilyn you now know of course but a real head turner and I thought wow Jim has struck lucky there, later on I discovered that she was shy and sensitive", she remembered.

" So When we made Gentlemen Prefer Blondes together and I discovered that she was nervous about going on set, I finally went to her dressing room and said: 'All right, baby, come on set with me now, we've only got a few minutes.' And she said: 'Ooh'". In the way she did you know and was fine I think what she lacked was a pal a gal pal and so I became that for her. I was very interested the Christian movement and while Marilyn had her own beliefs I think we got on well because of that you know, she trusted me and I her.

"What I recall though was the way Fox treated her I mean she was co-starring with me yet she was in the crummy dressing room and no real treats or anything. Zanuck I got the feeling still did not believe she was a star or maybe he just did not want to pay her you know so

anyway she would get upset over that but she never wanted to confront anyone so in a way it came apart because she kept it all inside " Janes then recalls "I remember the, Tommy Noonan who was a nice guy but like you know cocky and confident to a point and he had to do a kissing scene with her and you know he is kind of preening and all that like boys do, and afterwards some press guy asked: 'You've just kissed Marilyn Monroe. What was it like?' And Tommy replied: 'It was like being swallowed alive.' Marilyn overheard that and ran crying to her dressing room. No one could console her and let's just say that Tommy kept well out of the way after that.

Jane pointed out "Marilyn wasn't a dumb blonde she was an astute lady of many talents but she had an idea and went with it, I did tell her that she was playing with fire to keep the character up off screen but again the Press guys loved it that she went along with it you know. Marilyn though was very happy the last time I heard from her which was in 62 'Marilyn was planning to marry again, she told me this herself now maybe she changed her mind again as she was prone to doing but I know she loved Joe and he her. She told me that she figured he was only the true one the one that looked out for her you know so yes Right before she died, she was planning to marry Joe DiMaggio, her second husband, again, and she had a new movie contract with Fox she told me she was getting better deals and things were looking up, I mean Fox rehired her so that gave her confidence and while we spoke as she always did on aging she made me laugh because she told me "You know Jane I have lost weight but not on my figure in fact I think they have gotten bigger which made us both laugh out loud". So I don't think she killed herself.

Jane concluded that Marilyn's death was a case of "Someone did it for her. There were dirty tricks somewhere Its Hollywood they can create and cover up everything you know; how do we know what went on but I was behind Joe on not inviting all these people". Jane believed that both Jack and Bobby Kennedy - both Marilyn's lovers – could have been involved, look history will out it but if you crossed them well you knew it you know and I fortunately did not cross them but. Soon after Marilyn died, I ran into Bobby Kennedy and he looked at me as if to say: "You should be worried "I looked him straight back because I was frightened of no one and yet something stayed with me. Honestly apart from power what could she have seen in these people.

Eddie Fisher

He wed Liz Taylor and Debbie Reynolds - and threatened to shoot Richard Burton. The extraordinary life of Eddie Fisher had s strange connection to Marilyn Monroe and he revealed all when we met to discuss his tell-all book which turned out to be not quite so tell all really after all.

Five-times married Fisher, who died aged 82 at his home in California of complications from hip surgery, was famous for the women in his life. His first wife, Debbie Reynolds, was the much-loved star of Singing in The Rain (their daughter Carrie went on to make her name playing Princess Leia in Star Wars) and then there was Liz Taylor, who in 1959 stole Fisher from all-American sweetheart Debbie. It caused a huge scandal in Hollywood and compounded Fisher's reputation (he also enjoyed a string of romances with stars including Joan Crawford, Edith Piaf and Zsa Zsa Gabor).

Eddie was born in Pennsylvania in 1928, the son of poor Russian-born Jewish immigrants, Fisher's bell-like melodic voice was obvious in childhood. He won several talent contests and his father referred to him as 'Sonny Boy' after the Al Jolson hit record. He quickly became one of the earliest teen idols and as he told me "I was a real threat to Sinatra and he knew it but back in the day you were not allowed to attack other stars in print as it was deemed bad form.

In 1955, at the height of his career, Fisher settled down with Debbie Reynolds and they became Hollywood's favourite couple - until Liz Taylor came along.
Taylor was married to Fisher's best friend, producer Mike Todd, and the two couples spent much time together. When Todd was killed in a plane crash in 1958, Reynolds sent her husband to comfort the distraught Taylor. He never came home, and they married in 1959.

Fisher threw himself into furthering Taylor's career - putting his own on hold. When she was cast in Cleopatra, he travelled to Rome to be with her - setting himself up in a villa as her house-husband.

But he never counted on the effect her co-star Richard Burton would have and, when they met, dismissively said Burton's head was too large for his body; his legs too short and his face pitted with acne scars. He was also an angry drunk.

Yet after rumours emerged of Taylor and Burton's increasing friendship, Fisher told a press conference that the stories were 'preposterous, ridiculous and absolutely false'

He was so heartbroken that he thought he would never fall in love again. That is, until he spotted singer-dancer Ann-Margret on ¬television and invited her to ¬perform alongside him. But he shared her affection with none other than President Kennedy and Fisher demanded she chooses between them. She picked JFK. Fisher also had romances with dancer Juliet Prowse, Kim Novak and Frank Sinatra's future wife Mia Farrow. He claimed that being married to Liz Taylor had improved his life: s everyone assumed he must have something special to have ensnared such a legendary beauty.

In his biography, he also confessed to a drug addiction that lasted 40 years - blaming the use of cocaine for the decline in his career. Condemned to taking jobs in small venues to fund his habit, he found himself unable to remember the words of many hit songs. But Eddie was a fighter and still had charm in abundance but as with all my Marilyn connections what he revealed shocked even me as he blurted out "Neil let me tell you Marilyn Monroe was a serious player. She used people and I mean that in a nice way but she honestly never told anyone everything about herself she played them off and I know this for a fact as I was a victim of this too".

Eddie was in fine form but as he revealed to me Marilyn was insanely jealous of Elizabeth Taylor's fame and more so beauty he revealed to me "I knew Marilyn from way back when she started out with Johnny Hyde. She was a hustler you know a cute kid and all

*that but truthfully and this is lost in the mystery of her myth as soon
as she had dispensed with you were gone, finite, the end it's the way
she worked but nothing wrong in that we all did the same but with
her she was clever crafty and of course very switched on with whom
she should be associated with " Eddie took a long breath and
continued " You people forget how much Johnnie Hyde did for her
and while it's not know she did not want to marry him because while
he was mega rich she would have been a wealthy widow but maybe
not a movie star and that is what she really wanted that was her goal
and she made it but I was not surprised she ended up along because
it was almost a reality.*

*Eddie who was quite ill at this point told me he wanted to be blunt as
"I know the creation of myth around her is great and I am not
knocking that but let's not forget no one in the world of Hollywood
gets ahead by been nice, Marilyn whom I first met at the start of the
50's made a beeline for me and asked me on many occasions to date
but truthfully she was not the Marilyn creation then. Pretty yes but
fake and there lies your problem you see the people that fascinated
her were the like of Ava Gardner and Liz of course. Why? Because
they were genuine beautiful girls and Marilyn told me this herself "I
know I am a manufactured look the blonde hair and makeup I get it
but I also hope I give some hope to the ordinary girls like me who
maybe not the greatest beauty but this can be achieved and with luck
success too".*

*Eddie told me her fascination with Liz reached a peak when Marilyn
was dating Sinatra in the early 60's and all had been invited to see
Frank in Las Vegas with his special act. Eddie continued "So were*

sat together at a table with myself and Liz and Marilyn and some of Frank's pals. Now Marilyn arrives late to the table, unsteady on her feet and already a bit loaded with booze but not enough to forget the impact she was having on the room…. It was always about her and the effect she could create when she entered a room".

Eddie laughed and told me "Watching two of the world's most celebrated women in Marilyn and Liz be cordial to each other was a great experiment for me as you would have never guessed they loathed each other or indeed were any kind of rivals as with smiles and hugs you got the impression they were the very best of friends…".

Eddie at this point informed me that he was still married to Liz although he knew of her affair with Richard Burton at this stage and began to rant about that but as he stated " She knew at this point it was better to stay with me as Burton had at this stage no intention of leaving his wife Sybil to hook up with Liz but as he stated " It was the worst kept secret in Hollywood at this stage " It was at this point that Eddie said that Marilyn shocked even him with her suggestion as he added " she was between husbands as they say in Hollywood and so when we were in the interval of the show she was very friendly and kept kissing me and touching me and then she dropped the bombshell " Imagine what the people would say if we were found out to be having an affair ? Eddie laughed out loud telling this story but admitted "she was deathly serious as she knew that this would take the flame of interest right off Elizabeth".

Eddie added "I scolded her about this suggestion but she was very keen to pursue and told me her bungalow number for later that evening and when I mentioned she was Sinatra's date she just shrugged and said "If you like me you will come along".

Eddie did not want to elaborate on the rest of the evening but did let out some amazing facts about Marilyn and the Kennedy's " They owe her a great deal more so Robert than Jack because it was thanks to her intervention with Fox that they took up his idea of " The Enemy within" she was a fixer in that deal, It was well known at that time but also she was so enamoured with the Kennedy's she was deluded to think she could become part of their group you know the secret sect and all that but she really got used by people like Peter Lawford and all of his cronies...".

Eddie added that "Marilyn spoke with me about how she may marry again and how they may be in politics. She was quite mad in many ways but again she had already married two greats so why not a hat trick laughed Eddie.

Eddie surmises that it had to happen really in his words " I could not see where she would go next I mean she looked great sure she had lost lots of weight and regained her figure but you can't be young forever and she knew that I mean she knew her value was her looks and like every time she stepped out the critics are looking for tell-tale signs of ageing but this is before surgery took off I mean I think she would have been addicted to that if it was available at that time for sure because she was just that vain".

We finished the chat and Eddie did say he was stunned that she had become an icon and that it would have left her rather stunned too because "She really had no idea how popular she was I mean she loved been a movie star and all that but she had no real sense that she was popular because the studios made sure you were kept down. Eddie thought for a moment and finished with "I think it's interesting because in a way she has outlived so many others and really if you like without trying so maybe she was bright after all".

Debbie Reynolds

She is best known for her boundless energy and pert demeanour, legendary actress Debbie Reynolds has made memorable parts of superb films like 'The Tender Trap, ' 'Singin' in the Rain, ' 'Tammy and the Bachelor' and 'The Unsinkable Molly Brown. The actress who made her name opposite Gene Kelly in the screen smash

Singing in The Rain, was at the heart of the glamorous showbiz set in the Fifties, alongside Marilyn, Frank Sinatra, Bette Davis and Judy Garland.

I got to meet the legend for the first time while she was in London preparing for her one women show in the West End but as ever it turned out to be a rather strange meeting...Debbie had called a press conference to PR the show at a low-grade hotel in the heart of London but it all became clear when I met the producer who was putting on the show. You see you expect legends to hold such events in such grand places like The Savoy or Dorchester but this producer was known here in England for putting shows on that were to be kind carbon copies of other successful formats. I did wonder if she knew of his reputation but this slackness in a way gave me such great access as the producer along with his hairpiece and fake tan decided it was more about him and his reality show than actually helping to promote a legend on stage here. So much so myself and a cameraman found ourselves left alone in the suite with Debbie.

Having never met her before I was struck as just how pretty she was and polite but what was more fun she kept looking at this new tiny state of the art camera we had set up and asked "Are you sure this will film us and make us look good? She seemed fascinated that it may not capture it all but then she added "You see at MGM we had such huge cameras following us around and I know I am old-fashioned in thinking this but I do worry it won't capture us all to our best. It did and she was great I mean really nice and down to earth playing along helping promote the teaser for the show and just been generally a star so we got talking naturally about Marilyn and she told me this.

Marilyn was a bright girl you know but also many things to many people. I think the best way to describe it would be she applied herself to be what people wanted her to be. It's hard to explain but I am sure you understand you see to me she was a very kind soul, quiet and not at all movie star but then to someone else she could be bawdy and fun playing to the person she thought that person wanted her to be but I liked her I really did".

Debbie was relaxing and added "I think for her you know she knew she had a beauty and that was her thing but she also had talent and back then you were controlled by a studio and for her that was Zanuck at Fox. He was ok to me you know I liked him but again you have to remember Hollywood was a small town back then and all your secrets were not secret for that long because people gossiped so we knew all about Marilyn and her men. I think she was struck by people's education really I knew she liked that about Miller I mean what else could it have been really? Away from all the bright lights Debbie was able to see a very different side to the Misfits star, who was found dead at her Los Angeles home at the age of 36.

"We knew each other well because we attended the same church. Marilyn was very religious, which may surprise some people", she says. "It was very important to her and I think that it helped her many times in fact I knew it did as she told me it was the one constant in her li8fe that had not let her down "She would attend the

church very low key I mean again she could switch her persona on and off so you never really knew if she was there or not".

Debbie said "Often we would discuss the service and what it meant and how helpful that had been but I did see the depressed side of her personality but she always wanted to leave you on a high as it where I mean she was concerned for me as a single mother with two children she always asked about the children. I do think having a child would have maybe saved her because at her age of thirty-six she effectively was on her own and she knew it".

Debbie, went on to tell me says that she even warned Marilyn that her relationships with John and Robert Kennedy were putting her at risk". She would not listen because like us all in Hollywood we believe we know what we are doing best and with whom so while she kept it secret I knew as did everyone that she was the latest thing their play thing but only we could see that. "I saw her two days before she died she looked wonderful, super slim and very girlish so all the stuff you read about her been depressed and washed up were not true because if that was the case that she was doing a brilliant acting job of hiding that".

Debbie sat back in her chair of the hotel and sighed then told me "I warned her to be careful. With them the Kennedy's because they just used people I mean Joe Kennedy was known for it and why or why would they want to take that on board I mean she was a movie star who in an effective was a creation and that was something that they both liked but once used like a tissue they thought she would just blow away.

She was such a sweet and innocent girl but she was used by men. I believe she was murdered because too many people were afraid the truth would come out". I pushed Debbie on this as to hear someone so vital actually say that it was shocking but she added "When you look at the evidence and the time it took. The way people messed around in that vital time when she was dying well none of it stacks up but I guess we will never know the truth not until we all get up there and find out for ourselves "(pointing to heaven) 'For all her fame and beauty, men took advantage of her and she paid the ultimate price Debbie says.

Jerry Lewis

The legend that is Jerry Lewis rose to fame as Dean Martin's comedic partner, and his slapstick humour carried the multitalented performer through decades of film, television, stage and radio shows. After his split with Dean Martin, Jerry Lewis went on to a successful solo career as both an actor and director. His first film without Martin, The Delicate Delinquent (1957), was a huge hit and immediately established Lewis as a star in his own right. In 1959, Lewis signed a new contract with Paramount that paid him $10 million up front and 60 percent of box office profits, the most lucrative contract ever signed by a film star at that time. The contract also provided Lewis with greater control over his films, and he made his directorial debut with the 1960 comedy Bellboy I am telling you this as he told me this before we had even got going on our interview and yes he had some great Marilyn stories too hence he is in the book.

I met Jerry though through determination while he was appearing to great success at the Adelphi Theatre in London starring in the comedy musical "Damn Yankee's "Truthfully I was never that much of a fan before this but once you saw just how magical he was up on stage and how he lit up the stage with his sheer force of personality I was hooked and seen almost all of his films since meeting.

Jerry though was a tough nut to crack and admitted to me that he was of course a huge star log before Marilyn came onto the scene but was honest if nothing else "I think for those of us who have had a long life you know it's tough because we know just how these people, our friends have lasted in the fame game and its gets you wondering who will remember you like that you know. Marilyn was unique no two ways about it.

Jerry added " she was great had super comic timing and it was all an act you know the whole little girl thing so I am not so sure why she expired as such but having to create that every time you went out in public must have been tiring but at first she loved it because she had no idea of fame " Jerry added " she came on our radio show as a guest star when she was just getting going and loved it I mean she really took to the fact for her radio was great because while we had an audience which she thrived off for her it was super because she could hold a script so no lines needed to be learned and that was her fear you know lines".

Jerry states that while Marilyn was shy she was also very perceptive in many ways offering suggestions to the script that many others would not for instance Jerry says "she would say look you could get more comic value out of her here if we do this and so forth so she knew.

that it was a role she was playing that Marilyn was a creation and maybe one of the greatest creations of all time when you think about it in terms of movie icons.

Jerry though admitted that he was a nut to turn down the role that created one of the biggest films of all time "Some like it Hot "Why did Jerry Lewis turn down Jack Lemmon's role in 1959's "Some Like It Hot"? "I would have had a chance to kiss Marilyn Monroe", Lewis said, "Instead, [director Billy] Wilder called me 'The schmuck who turned down 'Some Like It Hot' for the rest of his life, and Lemmon [who was nominated for an Oscar for it] sent me chocolates every year until he died." But Jerry was quick to point out and graciously I felt that " I don't know if I could have done that better I mean it was a great pairing and Marilyn loved the role despite what you may have read but I know she signed on because she and her husband were broke at that time " Jerry denied to me that he refused the role because he did not want to wear drag " The truth is I was an idiot because at that time I had this great deal with Paramount and was the hottest things comedy wise in the movies so I know really I was checking my ego and all that .. Plus, Frank Sinatra was offered the role and I know like me he felt he would not be that convincing as a woman which was vital to the movie so maybe I made the right choices. Who knows, you can't go back, can you?"

Jerry though insisted to me that Marilyn Monroe never ever had that famous affair with President John F. Kennedy. He is serious about it too. Lewis says she didn't do it with JFK because…she did it with him, Jerry. He doesn't quite explain the reality of his story and what you have to remember with old time Hollywood stars is that they also know the vital role of upping their PR but Jerry continued of what could have stopped MM from, you, know, making love to the president and to him as well Lewis told me that the greatest sex-symbol used sex "to make an emotional connection". She used you basically because he knew she was hot you know so for her I think the only way she truly knew you liked her if that happened and it did for us".

Jerry states that he was shocked and saddened when he heard the news about the famous glamour gal but Hollywood should not be blamed. "After she had gone you read all sorts of stuff about the studios and Hollywood but let me tell you this Marilyn Monroe loved been a movie star she really did and enjoyed all the trappings that came with it". Looking relaxed he continued "the thing is there is no training book to tell you how to deal with things, your young and want fame well she got it but like so many she paid a hefty price and that was the shame of it all as I miss her every day she was a vital person and there are not many about".

Johnnie Ray

One of the greatest of the singers between the crooners and the rockers, Johnnie Ray was the only son of Elmer and Hazel Ray. He was born and raised in Oregon where he loved hiking in nature. He was close with his older sister, sometimes hiking with her. Mother nature eventually would inspire the song lyrics he wrote. After he had become famous, he corrected any reporter who asked him whether he preferred living in Los Angeles or New York. He insisted Oregon always would be his home.

Ray lost a large part of his hearing at age 13 in an accident while at a Boy Scout event. His hearing loss was not known to his immediate family for several months; they knew only that he became more withdrawn. After high school, he began singing locally in a wild, flamboyant style, unlike any other white singer up to that time. At age 25 he became an American sensation. The following year, during his first concert tour of the United Kingdom, Ray started attracting mobs of young people who rioted in front of him which predated the Beatles era. In 1954 he signed a deal with Fox and co-starred with Marilyn Monroe in the classic "There's No Business like show Business".

I met Johnnie towards the end of his life when he was touring here in the UK as part of a package style show, fun and friendly he told me he knew who I was going to ask him about as it was just two people that always came to the interviews with him. Marilyn Monroe and Judy Garland "People are simply fascinated by these two ladies and yet and I am not sure why because when you think about it they would be as stunned as we are talking about them in such detail "Johnnie was by this stage quite ill but had some great memories of working with Marilyn on the movie and remembers "we began shooting the movie on May 29th 1954 as I will never forget this date due to my nerves arriving on the Fox lot…I bumped into Marilyn on the first day and she was divine but also a bit gossipy she told me "I am only doing this lousy movie because I turned down another movie so you could say I am being punished "Johnnie recalls "she looked nothing like the sex bomb you would expect at all I mean her face was covered with Vaseline. Really covered though and she had no bra on and some old clothes " Johnnie asked her why she was covered in this gloop and revealed " I wear it when I am not working as it keeps my skin looking young " Johnnie told me " I had never heard of this but she had a lot of quirks like that for instance she was not a drinker you know despite what was written she liked Coke and coffee but mainly back then which was rare she drank a lot of water as she told me also " You have to look after your investment and mine is my face and figure so she knew what she was selling and what was on offer to others as it were ".

Johnnie said that Marilyn was very frightened of Ethel Merman because as she spoke loudly about this "Marilyn's role was not in the original stage version but Fox wanted her in for the box office. I told them I am box office "But as Johnnie added "No one dare speak up as she was loud and would have a go at you without the slightest hesitation so really I understood how Marilyn felt but at this point she was the biggest star on the Fox Lot if not the world yet she was treated quite badly by the studio I thought".

Johnnie revealed that when shooting had started Marilyn was already ill but the director Walter Lang kept pushing ahead and did not believe that she had a cold or whatever she was ailing at that time I think he just wanted to get the movie made quickly and move on but Marilyn had been offered a tease at this point also because in order to get her to do the movie they had lined up Billy Wilder to direct her in " The Seven Year Itch " which she really wanted to do and so played ball in part of that".

Johnnie remembers that Marilyn was the one who took time out with him to go over scenes and help even if she was not in his scene he recalls "she was totally sweet like that I mean she did not have to do that at all but she made sure I was looked after and I wanted to learn so I think she really related to that and we became firm friends "Johnnie adds though she had her own team also Natasha her drama coach whom he remembers as "Very nice but a drama coach not really. She seemed to gush platitudes to Marilyn which was basically "You're a genius you're great I wish there was more of you "and so forth so Marilyn I am sure kind of bought all that stuff up you know believed it yet the scenes were hardly dramatic stuff really".

Jack Cole was Marilyn's dance teacher and he was just great with her, helpful friendly and really cared about her in a way I think you can tell up there on the screen but Marilyn missed a lot of rehearsal time which did not go down well with the rest of the cast and crew. The thing is he recalled "You know the scene at the end of the movie where we all descend the steps while singing the song. Well we had all rehearsed and done it countless times yet she had missed them all. "Johnnie now starts to laugh at this stage as he remembers "So Walter the director shouts action and remember Marilyn has not done any of this but as we emerge on screen as it were she is perfect in time and smiling plus singing along to the backing track not one foot out of place. We did three takes in the end and each time she was perfect but she told me afterwards "I don't worry about things like that it's the dramatic stuff that worries me I enjoy singing and dancing "Johnnie added "Let's just say everyone on the set that day was thinking it was going to be Marilyn who messed up but not the case she proved to me what a star and performer she was just on that scene".

Johnnie also told me that Marilyn was not too bothered about her singing too as her deal with her record label meant that on the soundtrack it was dubbed so once Marilyn found this out she lost even more interest in the movie".

Johnnie who admitted to me he felt was a lousy actor says the reason she was so great is that she gave her all really to the minutes on screen and was highly visible you know you could not take your eyes off her on the screen and this was the same with her on set, whatever she was doing she drew you like a light to her really " Johnnie also remembered that Marilyn was very much in love with Joe DiMaggio but that he only came to the set once and this was on a fateful day when she was filming the heatwave number but as he remembers " I thought he was a bit of a sourpuss to be honest ... Now looking back as an older man I can see what bothered him really was the fact she was young and looking at worldwide fame and his if you like had been and gone so in a way he was more of an escort and this was not something he was happy doing but I think she loved him for sure. She did everything she could to make him happy and feel like he was vital but in the end I think his vanity won out".

Rod Steiger

Rod Steiger was an Academy Award-winning actor known for his roles in On the Waterfront and in the Heat of the Night. He trained at the Actors' Studio in New York City, emerging as an exponent of the Method, and made his Broadway debut in 1951 in Night Music. I remember meeting Steiger Outside the Langham Hotel in London quite by fluke as I was appearing at broadcasting House home of the BBC just across the road and decided to have a drink in the bar. Standing outside literally on the doorstep was the legend himself the star of "WC Fields and Me". And so many more. You would not have known him as a such but I have a photographic memory of real stars and he is one. I was quite nervous so I went up and I was with my mother also at the time and asked him "Do you mind if we get a picture together "He jumped back and said "Do you honestly know who I am you look so young "I loved him already and explained I was with my mother and that she was also a huge fan of his and that she was delighted.

He stood for the picture and told us both how angry he was at been kept waiting for a car to take him to the BBC. When I pointed out that the BBC was quite simply just there across the road he laughed and told me "Why the hell have they offered me a car then "he decided to saunter over and I offered to walk with him as he told me "I have no idea about the show or whom I am asking for".

So myself, mum and a Hollywood legend walked across to the world famous BBC Broadcasting house, while we were waiting Rod seemed fascinated about what me and my mum were doing here in

London and what we had been up to at the BBC. We told him I was a writer and broadcaster and explained that we had just been on a show and he was very interested in it all so much so after a while he asked if we would like to meet and have lunch after his studio visit. We were both stunned then it occurred to me that I could be paying for the lunch and Hollywood style that could be big bucks you know".

We met for lunch and he was divine really funny and open and generous and of course he began speaking about the famous method acting that he attended at the Lee Strasberg school in New York Rod remembers Marilyn well and told me she was rather odd to him at that time "she could walk through the streets of New York City and not be noticed and then, in a moment's time, make some inner adjustment to transform herself into the beautiful, breathy, and sensual movie star that everyone recognized. Heads turned, traffic stopped, and fans came running. "I just felt like being Marilyn for a moment, " she would say and Rod admitted to me that he thought she was an incredible actress just to be able to do that you know create that character on tap basically".

Rod explained why he thought Lee Strasberg got a bad rap from fans of Marilyn but they did not see how genuine she was about working with him and he her so you know they were both serious about their art "he added "I know he worked with her privately for three months at his apartment, tutoring her on the ability to grasp what was happening inside the character she was playing and then recreate that emotion inside herself. He also improved her powers of concentration and helped her break down scenes and scripts" he added "Once she had gained her confidence with herself which took a long time, she was allowed to join the regular classes at the Actors Studio, though she never became an official member. During her tenure at the Actors Studio, Marilyn focused on her craft with such intensity that she won the respect and admiration of many of her fellow students "they all liked her for sure but I think she took this like everything she did as a high school thing for her you know she was enjoying playing a new role may be that of a school pupil or something. I tell you think given the chance she would have become a great character actress and we all felt that in the studio and even for a while so did she".

Rod also told me that the Strasberg's, Lee and Paula gave Marilyn some much-needed confidence that helped her to believe in herself. The couple had faith in Marilyn's abilities and encouraged her goals. "For the first time, " Marilyn stated, "I felt accepted not as a freak, but as myself she told many people but Rod also pointed out "they were for a while her new family you know new ears. We are all hams us actors and Marilyn was really no different".

Rod though did let slip that Marilyn was very protective over any friendships outside of her own with respected pals and took him to task when Rod began a torrid affair with Miss Diana Dors.

Rod blushed as he told me "She came to Hollywood and landed a two picture deal with RKO and they were you know cheap shots really because they basically did not do the money but Diana was thrilled I mean this was her big dream plus she thought she was *taking on Marilyn who at the same time had gone to England to make a picture with Laurence Oliver.*

Rod sighed "Diana was a stunning lady but it was the wrong time and we were no great shakes as lovers I mean she was beautiful and kind all that but the truth is she had a lust for life and that was not me at that time I was into my acting and doing all the right things where as Diana was you know not a nice easy going lady at times because she had been treated badly by her husband Denis Hamilton. Anyway Marilyn got to know about my affair with Diana and gave me the third degree but she was really keen to hear if Diana was in anyway a threat to her status as the sex symbol of the time. I assured her this was not the case and all seemed well but Marilyn was not as easy going about rivals whatever you may have read about her".

Rod also hinted that Marilyn knew that she was a gay icon but was not that happy about it even then "she was stunned when I told her about Rock Hudson and she stated "But he has been married? "It was totally alien to Marilyn that not all men would not find her attractive and all that. She was always not too happy around gay men because she knew they could work her out where as a woman you know she could beat them simply with her figure".

Rod gave rare insight into how Marilyn felt about herself too explaining "she knew her talent if you like was built on her looks yet she did not believe she was beautiful at all she felt it was all manufactured she would say " I have fake blonde hair and I know my way around a makeup tray quite well so the only original thing about me is my figure and that is what I focus on because gravity will catch up with me one day " Rod revealed that she was quite clever when it came to herself in many ways " she knew she was a product of a studio and they could make her and break her so her idea of her own production company was not only ground-breaking given the time she did it but it was her saying I can be independent and I can make it without all you men.. Way ahead of her time".

As Rod departed it was an odd feeling to think that he had given so much of his memories but not long after the great actor passed away and I gave him a lot of thought because again he was a star and yet at that time he was almost forgotten. It got me wondering how Marilyn would feel thinking about all the stars that spoke of her and about her years after she was gone and how their fame was kept alive if you like by the flame of her enduring celebrity. Rod was very direct and honest but you do wonder how honest they would be if she was still around....

Buddy Greco

Buddy Greco began playing the piano at the age of four. As a child radio personality and gifted pianist he was a performing veteran by the age of 18 when he recorded his first hit 'Oh Look at Her Isn't She Pretty'. Buddy has sold millions of records and received gold records for hits such as 'The Lady Is a Tramp', and 'Around The World'. He enjoys rare distinction of having made 65 albums and 100 singles ranging in style from Jazz too Country/Western and Pop music.

The thing with Buddy is that he is a talented performer but like so many with a Marilyn association he is defined by that famous "last picture "of he and her prior to the tragic death and so far, Buddy never really gave out the story of what happened on what many fans called the "Lost Weekend" for Marilyn. Only Buddy knows what went on but again thanks to careful probing we can decide what is real and what is after many years a memory lapse on how to stay in the news if you keep an association going with a legend.

Uncertainty, contradiction and tragedy have always surrounded the mysterious and fateful weekend of July 28 and 29, 196 when you look at the cast list you can see why. Those who were there - including her on / off lover Sinatra (who had invited her personally to Cal-Neva), Dean Martin, Sammy Davis Jnr., Juliet Prowse (who was engaged to Sinatra), Peter and Pat Kennedy Lawford, and Paul 'Skinny' D'Amato, who managed the Cal-Neva Lodge for its owners Sinatra and his partner, the notorious Mafia godfather Sam Giancana - are either dead or still refuse to talk about what happened during those 48 hours. But Buddy knows and while still dapper and delightful I could not help thinking even now he was holding something back. Something vital that would give the final clue.

It's interesting to note at all that Marilyn went along because according to Dean Martin who told me "she was her own worst enemy in a way because she knew that Fox were mad with her for missing days and weeks yet there she was running around Vegas than getting ill time and time again "Dean added" I think many were stunned also because she was not keen on Juliet Prowse who was a great dancer and years younger than Marilyn. She kept asking me if she thought I thought her legs were as good as hers. It was that tragic in many ways because she felt this was the reason that Frank (Sinatra) had in fact moved on from her. In reality Frank had grown tired of all the drama in the life she brought with her".

In reality many people believe that even though w more than 500 plus books have been written about the life and death of the woman who was probably the greatest sex symbol of the 20th century, not one of them has managed to penetrate the mystery of Monroe's final days at Cal-Neva. Buddy Greco though himself a showbiz legend told me of meeting her there and what it was like.

"She was a vision I mean she did not look thirty-six you know she looked stunning but she was Frank's guest and basically when she pulled up in her car and stepped out she looked like the Monroe you saw on the silver screen the movies and all that "Buddy admitted that he felt she was "playing a role she knew she had to bring Marilyn to the party and not her real self which was Norma Jean she knew that for sure.

Marilyn was certainly in a terrible state at the time of her life. Robert Kennedy - who had inherited Monroe as a mistress from his brother, President John F. Kennedy - had just ended their five-month affair when she took off for Cal-Neva, As Billy Wilder pointed out "I was in contact with her after she got fired from Fox so I knew just how wild she was getting with her dreams. The poor girl thought that one of the Kennedy's would in fact marry her and you know I am not sure she was that bothered which one because by now reality was not a factor in her life and for her it was keeping as they say in today's terms her currency up there she knew that the Kennedy's could do that.

Buddy recalls of her demeanour weekend: 'She was fragile, very fragile - well, she'd gone.' A lot of people blamed the Kennedys but again we don't know what really went on because she was so fickle and could create a drama around her quite easily but she was distraught and heartbroken. She felt the Kennedys had handed her around and now had no further use for her which was a shame because many other gals in Hollywood took the same bait yet were not in her state, Frank Sinatra Jr also told me that according to his famous father "Her grip on reality - already weakened by her mental illness and worry about becoming like her mother plus drink and drugs - was certainly shaky.

As Buddy recalled that Marilyn also was fuming with Fox after the head of the Studio Peter Levathes had fired her and that he had done nothing to help her become a star yet had just dumped her in her mind " without warning " in his defence he claimed that her chronic absenteeism - in 35 days of filming, she had turned up a dozen times and when she did arrive she was so heavily medicated she could not remember her lines - he had fired her from Something's Got to Give, the film she was making with Dean Martin. But Marilyn had a problem with any man she could not control and this along with her worry about her looks fading and age did not help with the Kennedy situation .... He also issued a $500, 000 breach-of-contract suit against her and replaced her with Lee Remick. Its interesting to note also that Lee Remick whom I met told me she felt bad for years the way she was "used to try and keep Marilyn in check in that summer *of 1962 "I was so young, green and had no idea what she was going through yet I was a pawn and yes I had no plans to take over the role but I was contracted to Fox and they could get me to do anything they wanted really I was not in control at all".*

Marilyn though had something to smile about because her lawyers were in the middle of agreeing on a new deal with the studio and were confident that Something's Got to Give would resume filming in the last week of August, with Marilyn reinstated, but as everyone saw in the fatal weekend she was still drinking heavily and bingeing on pills, basically as Buddy puts it a "lost cause".

Buddy revealed that the weekend did not go great for Marilyn as she had a huge fall out with Frank Sinatra and while many may claim that this could have been because of his close friendship with the Kennedy's others don't quite believe that as Frank was never quite the same with them after the fall out over Jack's refusal to stay at the newly done up Sinatra home in favour of ageing crooner and rival Bing Crosby. As Buddy recalls "Frank was not a great forgiver as it were I mean if he fell out with you then that was it tragically as happened with Peter Lawford and many others but for me I knew how to keep Frank happy and that was the key to remaining friends basically.

Buddy though says he felt sorry for Marilyn "I got the feeling she was been used by so many. Fake friends and her willingness to comply were terrible really so after Frank dumped her and she had been escorted out of his showroom She was on my mind, ' he says. 'I was worried about her. I went outside to find out whether she was okay. I knew that she had taken accidental overdoses in the past and even though we were the same age at the time I was less mature and really had no idea how hurt and upset women can get. I mean I am sure I knew but in those days you did not get in touch with your real feelings as they say.

Buddy recalls 'I found her by the pool. There was nobody around. It was late and the pool was deserted. The ting I recall the most was the state of her I mean she looked like death so ghostly white and lacking in any colour at all. Almost like a ghost ' It could have been the slant of the moon. It still didn't occur to me that she might be a woman not long for this world she was just starting out to the lake swaying which also worried me because she was so banged out of it and not really there. We talked but I did not know if I was getting through at all I mean she was not responding in a normal way. Maybe her friends were used to seeing her like that but it worried me. Anyway, we talked and about all sorts of stuff and then I gently took her hand and walked her back to her room and said good night as she walked back into her bungalow" That was the last I saw of her because in the morning she had gone. "Buddy added "because the weekend was so busy and people were milling around plus the strange state of her appearance no one really questioned where she had gone or who and I dare not bring it up I mean its Hollywood these things happen.

Mickey Rooney

*Mickey liked to regale the story of how he found and named
Hollywood star Marilyn Monroe and even composed tunes for her "
she was beautiful but not stunning as she later became, Marilyn was
hanging around with an agent pal of mine called Johnny Hyde and
did so much work for her and it was him and me that decided the
path of her career honestly it's true I suggested that she be called
Marilyn after an old MGM star Marilyn Miller and he also came up
with the stories that she came up with for the press .... Mickey had
many tales like this and discussing them was always fun However
over many meetings. Interviews and phone calls her gave a rather
disturbing account of Marilyn's rise and fell into the world that
eventually led to her early demise.*

*Meeting Mickey Rooney for me was exciting as he was a true
Hollywood legend but again like all meetings and interviews it was*

one that was tinged with oddness really. I remember the day of our
first meeting, He was in town to promote something and I was
assigned by the news channel I worked for to interview him. The
thing I remember was clearly how he must have been struggling for
money as he was staying at a downmarket Hilton Hotel which billed
itself as Kensington but in reality was Shepherds Bush. An odd
location for one who had been a star for many years I am sure you
will agree.

Upon turning up at the hotel for the first time he ushered me in
personally but he had fallen out with his "current "wife called Jan
who was crying and wailing in the bathroom. I looked around the
room which was small neat but not a suite it was for someone who
was a single night business traveller and Mickey sensed this and
took hold of the situation " "We have had a mix up with the hotels
and we should have been in the Hyde Park but this lousy place was
all they had left so I am not very happy " I noted this but looking
around the room I also noted that if this was the case the Rooney's
had settled in and seemed quite happy to be there so I assumed that
maybe money was a bit tight ... Mickey had requested cash for the
interview and I had refused as I told him "We are a news channel
you're promoting that is the deal "He accepted it but before his wife
came out of the bathroom he asked me again for money as he wanted
to put some on the GG's and when I explained again I don't give out
money he sulked".

Having spent a lot of time with him over the years many refute a lot
of his claims about his close association with Marilyn but you have
to remember he was there and not us plus he had some very good

back up including letters and pictures that I have never seen since so whatever you think he did know her quite well over the stardom period of her life and he insists that he discovered "Norma" at a party given by the bandleader Ray Anthony, and that he later suggested she change her name because, "You're definitely a Marilyn, " and also because just moments after this historic moment he received a call from his "writer friend Monroe Manning". When I disputed this and said well the story goes is that Norma Jean's name was changed after she signed her first contract with 20th Century Fox in August 1946. Her mentor at the studio, Ben Lyon, thought of "Marilyn" because he was fond of the stage actress Marilyn Miller, and Norma Jean suggested "Monroe, " her mother's maiden name.

The party Mr. Rooney recalls was actually held six years later to commemorate Marilyn Monroe's ascent to superstardom in "Niagara". The event is captured on film and shows Monroe arriving by helicopter, Mickey Rooney playing the drums and Ray Anthony crooning his original composition "Marilyn "Again though Mickey dismisses this as something the studio created as "I was not hot at that time and they would not want their rising star been associated with a has been as I was seen back then as me but I am telling you the truth".

Mickey who had been married eight times by then also confessed to an affair with Marilyn and he was very frank and brutal in his appraisal of her "she was even then angry at how another of my exes was in the beauty stakes. Elizabeth Taylor so that is really how we got connected I mean again people dispute this because they read all the fan magazines but what happened when Louella and Hedda went to bed is another matter and Marilyn was so interested to learn just what made Liz so popular with the men and that she as going to be totally different and learn something new that would appeal to men.

Mickey added "she used men I mean I was useful to her I could get her invited to parties, I knew people and she knew that I knew people. We talked marriage as I like been married as you may have gathered but seriously she was that keen. Not on me but the idea of marriage and when we made the "Fireball "together she was hounding me then to get engaged and announce it but all the while she spoke of many other men as well I was very aware of all that but she did not hide it also, she loved the power she had over men but then I introduced her to Joe and that was that really".

I saw Joe "recalled Mickey and started paying homage to great DiMaggio. Marilyn Monroe, a young starlet on the way to fame herself, was instantly impressed and captivated by the power of Joe DiMaggio's mystique, several years after he had retired from baseball she asked me "who is that "I explained that it was the greatest baseball player ever and then for that moment on she decided he was more use and I was always the good short friend who once had a movie career "he laughed.

Mickey states that Joe was the "love of her life "but you see with Marilyn she played scenes so she became the ideal wife with Joe doing the dishes, walking, hiking and playing baseball even with him, I don't think she was not in love with him but she easily grew tired of playing that role and then she needed a new shot. A bit like a drug addict you might say who needs to know what she can get next to keep the high going "Mickey and Marilyn often talked about the perils of fame and he told her how he felt trapped in his child-like body. "I was a 14-year-old boy for 30 years, " he stated. It became a curse he could not escape. When I was 19 I was the No 1 star. When I was 40 nobody wanted me "He insisted that Marilyn told him it would not happen to her as she was developing a duel personality so that "I can just switch it back and forth as and when its needed".

Mickey in his career amassed two honorary Oscars, four Oscar nominations, an Emmy and two Golden Globes in a nine-decade film career. His hit movies ranged from 1944's National Velvet with Elizabeth Taylor and Breakfast at Tiffany's with Audrey Hepburn, to Ben Stiller's recent trilogy of Night at The Museum comedies. But he admitted "I don't get the respect like others do I mean what makes Marilyn a legend .is it because he was tragic like Judy or was it her acting and films. I am not sure but I do know that she thought of herself as a joke in many respects because she told me "I have at best fifteen years at this because as soon as I am old no one will want me but maybe I won't be around by then "Mickey says he never knew how serious she was about her life or indeed suicide because "she talked about it a lot she was depressed an awful lot and felt you know that life was hard and she was going nowhere but then she would click on the Marilyn persona and be away.

Mickey also revealed that Marilyn had developed another crush towards the end of her life that of Peter Falk famous as that coat wearing detective "Columbo". Mickey lets this gem out "she knew of him because she always took note of new men in the business and about possible co-stars, she even liked the idea of him co-starring with her in the movie 'Let's Make Love' but she found her friendship with him again in 1962 and spoke about him to me again and said he was "perfect", which of course he was not but to Marilyn he was ideal as she could dominate him on screen".

Anita Ekberg

Although Anita Ekberg did not win the Miss Universe pageant, but as one of six finalists she did earn a starlet's contract with Universal Studios, as was the practice at the time. This of course led to an iconic career as a sex symbol and as studios loved at that time European starlets she was on a role to great success.

Anita Ekberg was indeed a teetering tower. She was 5ft 7in tall and possessed a considerable bust, of which she once said: "It's not cellular obesity, it's womanliness". Ekberg showed that she could really act, if given the opportunity, when she played Hélène Kuragin, the unfaithful wife of Pierre Bezukhov (Henry Fonda) in King Vidor's epic War and Peace. However, she was fully aware that her allure was centred on her physicality. "I have a mirror", she said in the late Sixties, "I would be a hypocrite if I said I didn't know I am beautiful". Anita was and remained a huge icon to beauty but she was rather honest with me about her rival of beauty Marilyn Monroe.

"I get asked that a lot about her but we can never be honest because we sound bitchy. To me she was great and rather ahead of her time when you think about it, I mean she started her own production

*company, made movies and was not dumb at all but the true thing is
sadly she died young so she remains well a true beauty, I totally
loved her and she was a bit older than me but again I thought she
was someone to admire and work towards. I don't know the real
story behind her last years but you know she should have returned to
the baseball guy because he loved her without a doubt and that to
me was worth anything more than a few awards and career".*

*Anita thought was honest and stated "I think also people forget she
was a great operator people forget that also she had rivals of which
I was not one but Jayne Mansfield joined Marilyn as a Twentieth
Century-Fox contract player in the 1950s. Though a clever
comedienne and a shrewd self-promoter, Jayne you know lived
forever in Marilyn's shadow and I know that hurt her but unlike
Marilyn she was not an original.*

*From the moment Jayne arrived onto the scene in the Broadway
version of Will Success Spoil Rock Hunter? She was compared,
contrasted, and sometimes even equated with the world's most
famous blonde. Like Marilyn, she had a burning ambition to become
a movie star, and she laboured to build her own image through
outrageous publicity stunts but you need talent and Jayne frittered
hers away when you think about because again like all of us girls at
that time we were governed by men who ran the studios. What could
we do?*

*Anita added "I was told by critics that I lacked Marilyn's touch of
innocence and flair for comedy but that was never my plan so again
you can see like Marilyn how much the studios decided our path.*

Anita concluded with "You know I think in the final year of her life I have never seen anyone more beautiful than Marilyn. She really shone and looked stunning which always makes me think she had so much more to give but again she lives on through her glorious image which really is all any of us can ask when your labelled a sex bomb".

Chris Lemmon (Son of Jack)

I met Chris Lemmon in the summer of 2016 and went along to see his one man show which was getting great reviews for the first time ever staged in London, Chris came along to the studios and was a blast from start to finish and we really go on. You know sometimes you meet people in this world of showbiz and while you both know the deal i.e. You are there to plug their product well with Chris we really hit it off and I was delighted to see him doing so well on stage later that week but like all children of Hollywood's mega stars he was and continues to be amazed at the love for his father all these years later and of course we chatted about his role in the now iconic " Some Like It Hot " which Chris revealed " Dad loved that movie and had a far different relationship with Marilyn say that Tony (Curtis) Dad told me " I loved her I thought she was terrific and

such an accomplished actress but her own demons got in the way but on the good days she was well like no one else " Chris also was lucky enough to meet Marilyn and recounted a lovely story of how he knows for sure that there was a " relationship " with Jack Kennedy " I had snuck into a back garden that was been used for a party and in that party in the pool no less was Marilyn and the President which would have been in the early summer of 1962 so whatever stories you hear I know as a young boy what I saw and while I got told off by my mum you know it was obvious that they were an item " Chris admits he feels that " No one could have saved her really because no one saw it coming I mean she was the world's biggest star and time and time again she had been knocked but the fans loved her and what she stood for so what was not to like and even when her studio fired her Fox had to admit in the end that there was no one quite like Marilyn " Chris told me that of course he was a bigger fan of his own father Jack and he revealed ""He was my best friend, "Losing your father really stinks. "Of course now, Lemmon gets him back again for 90 minutes each night, and matinees on weekends, as his show has taken many parts of the world by storm, I asked him if it was hard reliving his past nightly on stage in full of strangers but he happily admits "No not at all, this way I feel better connected than ever and the love that I have felt back here in London has been wonderful truly, I think Dad and Marilyn would be thrilled to know they are still even to this day so loved the world over.

Ricci Martin

Dean Martin was just one of those amazing guys — an entertainer who transcended genre, an icon whose work spanned decades, quintessentially cool before cool was even hip. But to young Ricci (pronounced "Ricky") — the second son with Martin's second wife, Jeanne, and the sixth of Martin's eight children — Dean Martin was just Dad. Ricci came to London to perform in his one man show and naturally we invited him on the chat show to talk about his life and career but what was really interesting to me was that he of course as a young boy witnessed Marilyn at the very end of her life and with her on going troubles with Fox and "Something's Got to Give" which co-star his father Dean.

Meeting Ricci who was so very handsome and a natural entertainer was a great thrill. While he was in the green room and chatting prior to filming the show he seemed normal, easy going and nothing really like his famous father that is until we announced show time and he slipped on an elegant sports jacket and he suddenly became a "star" more so he became the double of Dean right down to the way he sat and moved...

Ricci recalled at great length how and what happened during that difficult time of Marilyn's battle with her studio "She was for me the ultimate women I mean she glided into our living and I know she loved coming to see Dad as he had a very much family oriented home set up, she would sit down next to me and if I was playing with something like a toy or whatever she was you know keen to get involved. I think looking back Children would have helped her a great deal because she related to them and likewise I did to her she was always ladylike and very fragrant. She always smelled like a lady I do recall that and there was nothing of the brassy type sex symbol that was portrayed in magazines "Ricci remembers "she listened to my father a lot regards her career and what to do but even I knew that only part of it was sinking in because and I say this kindly she went in and out of moods but now as an adult it may have been the stimulants she was taking but I know that she valued his word and he helped win back her deal with Fox".

Dad only wanted to appear in "Something's Got to Give "with Marilyn and no one else so he made sure she was invited back and he felt she was great in the movie but he I heard him telling my mother she was "afraid of looking old on camera and that this might just be it".

Ricci Martin, son of the world-famous singer Dean, was just like most any other teenager in the early months of 1962 but he fondly recalls "I can honestly say having spent time with Marilyn she really was my 'wake-up call' as a young boy she was everything to everyone and I know she loved the fact that she had this effect on me". She told me: "I think you look so cute when you blush Ricci", which of course he did every time they met: "she was more beautiful though and natural in many ways as she just had an air about her, you know; it was inbuilt and I think that is what the camera picked up on her natural way with her own body and she was happy to share that with the world".

Ricci though was lucky in many respects because he gave us a clear view on the state of Marilyn in the final few weeks of her life and the world she had become attached too as he recalled to me "Dad was furious with Fox because basically they loathed Marilyn and she had no idea just how much they loathed her, Reason? Well As Dad told me they were all new people around the studio and like all new people they wanted to make their mark plus they felt that Marilyn was over the hill, past it and that included my Dad but the main factor was she was cheap and easy to get as they had a film deal out of her and of course she was still Marilyn Monroe but on top of that Dad told me that the new boss Peter Levathes had zero ideas about making pictures because he was firstly an advertising man and then headed up Fox's TV output yet Dad was not so sure that Marilyn knew of his background at that time.

Ricci also pointed out that Dean had discussed with him how they were simply just mean to Marilyn in order to get her down and basically do what they wanted. She wanted her regular hairdresser that was decided as a no, she couldn't have her regular hairdresser. Whatever she wanted, the rule was, she couldn't have it. Dean saw more and more of it day by day, it became clearer and clearer what was going on—and then Dean overheard conversations about it between the executives, that is why he quit the production when she was fired simply because Dad was a kind man and knew that she was in an impossible situation but as I say I was a young boy and basically Dad told me this long after Marilyn had departed this world.

Ricci though explained how Marilyn would come over to the house on a regular basis and was far from depressed "She got on well very well with Dad and he had time for her and it showed. I never saw for a moment that she was depressed at all but I know she had lots of hangers on like the press women Pat Newcombe who was something of a dragon basically and also the housekeeper. I know she wanted rid of them because I would sit and listen to her telling Dad about how they spied on her. She actually said those words spied".

As Ricci relaxed and opened up he admitted that he thought Marilyn had a eating problem also towards the end of her life as she became the thinnest anyone had seen her and Ricci has a theory about this dramatic new look " My take on this is that Marilyn knew where the 60's were going, she was getting older and needed to reinvent herself with a new look and this worked well for her but whenever she came over to the house she always brought her own food which

*was always chopped liver, dried toast and boiled eggs plus
sometimes she would have chopped up pieces of pineapple also so to
me that was quite a drastic diet and my mother would cook for her
these things as she said the housekeeper kept forgetting to get food
in so Marilyn in effect had to so all her own shopping or cook it
which in turn led her to dislike the housekeeper a lot.*

*Ricci also admitted that Dean had no time for the producer of the
movie and someone again who loathed Marilyn Henry Weinstein, the
problem as Ricci was told by Dean was simply this "He had directed
one movie and suddenly he is directing two of the biggest stars in the
world and his inexperience was so obvious and for that Dean again
felt the movie was doomed plus he changed his story a lot over the
years to make out he was in fact on Marilyn's side which truthfully
he was not".*

*Ricci was fascinating in the people that he met in Marilyn's life,
people we read about but don't really know how they ticked at all
one was none other than Marilyn's celebrity doctor Dr Ralph
Greenson. Ricci described him as "creepy and very unsure about
everything around yet he kept a tight control over her and made sure
that she deferred to him for all sorts of silly dilemma's in her life
something again that really annoyed Dad.*

*Ricci goes on "One night he came to the house for Marilyn like he
was her boyfriend or something which I found rather strange, he
refused drinks and kind of hung around the hallway waiting for her
which got me thinking that she must have hated him just turning up
as she was having a good time with us and he came to ruin it". Ricci*

cleared up the mystery of Marilyn's hospital visit with her bruised face once and for all as he told me that Marilyn indeed confessed to Dean that it was Greenson that had hit her but "not to tell a soul Marilyn though would not have a word said against him and insisted that it was her fault on how it happened, Dad though had him removed from the set as he decided then that he could help direct Marilyn..." Ricci summed it up with Marilyn quite well he revealed "I think the true problem she was grateful and I mean grateful to anyone who would take her on so come 1962 she was thrilled when the Dr decided he could rescue her. But in truth I don't think anyone could".

Ricci noted that Marilyn, who hadn't made a film in 18 months, was consistently late or absent for days at a time; illness was the usual excuse. Director George Cukor shot around her, filming scenes with her co-stars, but after 30 days of production, 17 of which she had missed, she was fired. But again Ricci reveals that George Cukor loathed Marilyn. "He told dad that he did not like her at all but was quite a pansy and would you know gush to her to get her on time and all that but behind her back he truly was a nasty old queen and many people would say that if they were honest "Ricci reveals that" Dad was struck with the way Marilyn dealt with him. He said she effectively "gushed right back and confused him even more and of course it worked but again what a way to work when you're the world's biggest star".

Ricci recalls how upset his father was at the death of Marilyn and how he was banned from paying his last respects at her funeral " He loved her for sure and figured whatever problems she had could be worked out but I know that he was hurt to be spurned at her funeral because he told me so " Ricci recalls " It was silly now looking back but I know that dad felt Joe DiMaggio's grief was beyond anything he had seen and maybe he felt he could finally have control over the wife he lost but Dad went to grave often to leave flowers and remember her, Ricci added " He knew she was totally alone and that bothered him but this is way before she became a legend that really only happened towards the end of the sixties so yeah I know he dropped flowers and shared his private thoughts with her and we all respected that".

Ricci though did confess that all was not well with his father and Marilyn on many occasions as he was annoyed that she had agreed to go and appear at the famous President Kennedy Birthday party in which she famously sang " Happy Birthday " As Ricci explains " Dad had also been asked to perform but because of the movie he declined only to find out that she was going so yes there was friction in that respect as it was the biggest event of the year, well decade but Marilyn had in fact got approval from Fox at the start of the movie so no great shock for her and she seemed to easily glide over Dad's annoyance really.

Ricci did add that "Dad never was that clear on his reasons for putting his career and his future on the line for Marilyn, His loyalty to her though was far from popular. "Nasty sayings were scrawled on his dressing-room door", he told my mom about it remembered. "By insisting on Marilyn it seemed as if their movie would shut down for good – with the loss of one hundred and four jobs".

My Dad "added Ricci was not a fan of the studio head Peter Lavathes and even more so I remember he came back and told my mom all about the meeting which could in effect have had a bad time in his career in Hollywood but Dad told me also that he had taken the role mainly because "the chemistry between Marilyn and myself was right". He also said that the whole point of Something's Got to Give was Martin's desertion of his new bride, Cyd Charisse, for Monroe, which was something which wouldn't happen, Martin said, "with Lee Remick". Cue Lee Remick not having a go at dad in the press laughed Ricci...Dad was a really nice guy you know but by sticking up for Marilyn he did put a lot on the line and she appreciated it I know that also – In the end the studio had no choice because they were losing so much money anyway and he told Lavathes that. He would not do the film without Marilyn Monroe, and that was final.

Ricci told me that he believed that "something sinister had happened to her in the last few weeks and I for one don't believe she ever wanted to take her own life. There are many unanswered questions but you know she mixed with some high people and despite what Dad tried to tell her in many respects she was a loose cannon. She believed that the Kennedy's truly liked and loved her yet she had also seen the string of girls they have left behind so in reality why would she be any different.

Cyd Charisse

Long-legged, seductive and sexy, without a doubt she was one of Hollywood's iconic dancing stars, who along with Eleanor Powell, Ann Miller and Vera-Ellen. Were all quite superb Although she excelled in the balletic style, she could dance with the best, as she showed numerous times in her stunning gym dance, "Baby, You Knock Me Out", in It's Always Fair Weather, and her "Fated to be Mated" duet with Fred Astaire in Silk Stockings. Cyd was in London in the middle 80's to star in the musical version of "Charlie Girl "when I met her and of course while I adored her as a personality in her own right it was the fact had a supporting role that year in Something's Got to Give, the last, unfinished film of Marilyn Monroe. And I knew she would be full of great stories, "Charlie Girl" ran at the Victoria Palace theatre in London and was a huge success for Cyd who when I first met her was with her husband Tony Martin.

She was a very gracious lady who oozed beauty and style and while she was reluctant at first to speak of her time on "Something Got to Give "she relented as "I don't want to add more misery to Marilyn's story after all people have taken advantage of her and I have nothing but good things to say about my time with her. There is plenty of other juicy gossip, though. Monroe is lauded for her enormous charisma and often underappreciated skills as an actress as Cyd testified "she was brilliant I mean I was doing a comedy with very little skill and she was so helpful which is not ever mentioned or written about I mean the world's biggest movie wanted to know if I would like to run through my lines with her. That is and was so gracious she did not have to do that but for me I had trouble with George (Cukor) simply because in my opinion he had very little time for Marilyn and would make her do endless retakes which she did not complain about at all but truthfully I would have been very angry had it been me doing those time and time again.

I asked Cyd if she recalled this rumour about how Marilyn also cattily accused co-star Cyd Charisse of padding her bra so that her breasts would seem larger than the stars. "You know that is so not true and I think something the studio may have made up because and you can quote me on this she was great with other women on set and always paid them compliments about their hair, skirt or whatever she was a girl's girl alright and I if she did say that so what she was Marilyn Monroe famed for her figure and stunning beauty ...

Cyd recalls the time she appeared in the infamous swimming pool sequence " she looked beautiful to me though she looked a broken women I had heard she had been unlucky in love again and while she disguised it well she told me over the phone in one of our late night chats that she had been " badly let down " The thing is Neil it was not for me to ask by whom I mean she alluded to all that in our chats but I think she appreciated the point that I was not probing and prodding about something that had deeply upset her for sure". Cyd also pointed out that "Marilyn was taking her career very seriously I mean all she ate was chopped liver and boiled eggs because she wanted to look her very best on camera. This was a big deal for her yet I believe Fox had no interest in her at all other than making a quick buck and she was wise to this for sure I believe that because she told me "I don't want to work with Fox again she had problems with Gene Allen and others with the production. Cyd also cleared up the delays "Many were not her fault we did not have a clear script and like Marilyn I was worried this was not going to be a great film also remember Fox had not paid her salary for the movie so she knew that if it failed to ignite the box office they could easily blame her and maybe not even pay her she knew all this".

As we sat in her rather dismal dressing room at the Victoria Palace we discussed the theatre and its history which seemed to appeal to Cyd as she had no idea "I was going to be here and now I get to meet the Queen too "(Cyd would in fact go onto to me HM, The Queen Mother and the Duchess of York Sarah Ferguson. The Queen bypassed the Royal variety show that year) Cyd though was very kind and thoughtful of her one time iconic co-star " I don't ever think she would have believed she would have been this loved or remembered, she had a very little self-worth and yes I heard the story about my hair been darkened but that was my choice I loathed been lighter and you know Neil this was my first comedy role which was not about my looks so it was great not to have that pressure on me, again I would say that Marilyn was stunning throughout the picture and I thought she was most delightful in the role, Cyd also let slip that she and Marilyn had such a laughing fit on set when they were filming the scene where she plays the maid with her " Garbo accent " she was brilliant at it and was a great mimic in real life you know .. She could pick up accents really well and did an amazing take off of Larry Oliver from her time with him so when people say was she a good actress I would say no she was terrific but very little back then was seen of that " Cyd also pointed out that she and Marilyn had actually met way back in the late 40's at Dancing Ballet

Class " she was very good and very ahead of her time in terms of keeping fit and looking after her body and so forth people again forget she had such foresight but at ballet she was exquisite but people failed to take her seriously and then as we all know she became an icon so what did it all matter.

Cyd's prevailing memory of filming "Something's Got to Give "was not just the phony set of George Cukor's house but of course Marilyn's nude swim, Marilyn was making only $100, 000 for what would be her last film, Something's Got to Give, in 1962, while Taylor was receiving a million dollars for Cleopatra. She wanted to show Fox that she could get the same kind of coverage as the publicity bonanza generated by Taylor's very public affair with her co-star, Richard Burton. When Hugh Hefner agreed to pay $25, 000 for a nude shot of Marilyn—the most money Playboy had ever paid for a photograph—Fox and more importantly director George Cukor became interested Marilyn told Cyd. "There isn't anybody that looks like me without clothes on. "and as Cyd agreed " she was right you know I mean what she was doing for our movie was amazing when you think about it because this for sure was going to generate some great publicity and it did of course " Cyd agrees though that Marilyn was " very upset with Liz Taylor but on many levels Cyd reveals " I pointed out that both were so different yet unique and one could not do the other so really was what the issue but I think or at least she hinted that she thought Liz was a natural beauty and she felt she was rightly so " Not so natural but I am just a girl with a figure you know so maybe she has more to offer plus she has won an Oscar".

Cyd added Marilyn didn't have a preconceived idea of how she wanted to be seen by the public. All she wanted was to make sure that her face or body didn't appear blemished in some way: a line here or a wrinkle there. She was interested in the total image; She had so many beauty tips and secrets and they were way ahead of our time and some that I still use today, Cyd recalled how sad in parts Marilyn was during the filming of "Something's Got to Give "I think she loved been an actress but she told me "I never wanted to be Marilyn—it just happened. Marilyn's like a veil I wear over Norma Jeane, but you know and I now know this to be true. Fame is something you just can't switch on and off so I guess I am Marilyn for good now "Cyd told me she was so sad when she said this though.

I really enjoyed our time together Cyd was a gracious hostess and really nothing was too much trouble for her in respect of questions…Cyd told me "I don't think I will be remembered much but the fact I made a movie with Marilyn Monroe may make people take a look at me from time to time".

Jean Kent

A performer from age 11, Jean Kent was billed as Jean Carr when she danced in the chorus of London's Windmill Theatre, Kent made her first film appearance in 1935, hitting her stride in the mid-1940s. She joyously harked back to her music hall roots in the leading role of the 1945 movie musical Trottie True. A busy television performer, Jean Kent has been a regular on such British series as Sir Francis Drake (1962, as Queen Elizabeth), Tycoon (1978), Crossroads

(1981), Lovejoy (1990) and Shrinks (1991). Kent died in 2013 at age 92

Jean Kent, who appeared alongside Monroe in The Prince and the Showgirl, in 1956 she told me that the actress "never arrived on time" and forced a fellow actor to "take to drink" due to difficulties filming her scenes. Speaking with Jean who was a delight she confessed that she was more than harsh at her words on Marilyn but stuck by them " The thing is I was not a fan you see, what happened I suppose in a way was the green eyed monster I mean We, I had been the darlings of the Gainsborough films and all that then suddenly it was all well you know blonde hair and boobs as you say today" Jean was still a good looking gal when I met her but she did say that " To me she was well If you passed her on the street, you would never have thought: 'There goes the world's number one sex symbol but I agree she had something magical on camera but the thing I always smile about is her gay icon status simply because she treated Dickie (Richard Wattis) quite bad really I mean he took to drinking quite a bit because she was less than nice to him but she was not warm to " fags " as she called them I believe because she could not control them but now you know I think she would have loved to know the gay scene loves her so much but it was a totally different time in the 50's for that sort of thing you know, Jean told me "I know what it meant to be a star, and regarded it as my job to live up to that position and never to disappoint the public. Marilyn on the other hand had all this "method "nonsense going on and I believe that was the down side of her because looking at the film now she was delightful on camera".

Jean added that Marilyn was a genius in the sense "she became Larry Oliver's boss on the movie you see, something he could not abide but you would never have known she was the boss because she gave a lot over to him, quite generous in that respect but she was always aloof and then of course she would have Arthur Miller with her but it got easier once he hot-footed it back to the US she became more bearable and all that but again I am not sure just how in love she was with him".

Jean's abiding memory of Marilyn was that she was lonely "She really was I mean she never really mixed with us girls yet we were warm and friendly towards her and all that but she was always swept away by her fierce looking drama coach. She was a one you know she would gush and gush to her like she was the second coming which was very funny to hear but I did wonder if Marilyn actually believed all that she was been told because in a way as Larry told me "It's like speaking to someone under fog "Jean though admits "she was a troubled soul and I think truly unhappy but some people are just like that really I mean you can't help them because they live in that state don't they?

Rock Hudson

Rock Hudson has exceptional good looks and his comedic film performances, Rock Hudson was an iconic actor who, later in life, contracted and died from the AIDS virus.
Rock Hudson began his career as a sex symbol, many acknowledged his acting talent in Giant (1956), which also starred heavy-hitters Elizabeth Taylor and James Dean. He co-starred with Doris Day in

many hit films, including *Pillow Talk (1959), Lover Come Back (1961) and Send Me No Flowers (1964). In 1984, Hudson was diagnosed with AIDS. The following year, he became one of the first celebrities to disclose both his homosexuality and AIDS diagnosis. Hudson was the first major celebrity to die from an AIDS-related illness, on October 2, 1985, at age 59, in Beverly Hills, California.*

Rock was a good celebrity friend to Marilyn Monroe but admitted he regretted turning down the opportunity to co-star with her on a few occasions including the 1956 hit movie " Bus Stops " and her very last film " Something's Got to Give " I met and spoke with Rock on many occasions and he was a gentleman and more so a real Rock to pardon the pun as he spoke with great kindness about the many stars he had worked with but as he told me the final time he spoke to Marilyn he knew " It would not be long before a tragedy struck " One of the final times I saw Rock was at the BBCTV theatre in Shepherds Bush when he appeared on a chat show which was filmed there .. He was always divine and really revealing yet again it's only years later looking at notes and old tapes you realise what these stars were revealing to you because. One your very green and young and also you had no idea what they were speaking about but years and knowledge makes you pick up what they were shocking you with.

"The Thing with Marilyn "he told me in London while appearing on a BBC TV show "Was that she was always too steps away from something happening I mean she was very lonely in many respects but again she shunned many people who could have cared for her such was her deep mistrust of people. She much preferred as she called it the "ordinary Joe " because he believed they would not

hurt her " Rock admitted that it took some time for him and Marilyn to become friends because she refused to believe that he was gay and she was not keen on this aspect of his life " She really did not understand this side of things at all because she was used to men just falling at her feet and while homosexual men did it was for the different reasons so she was not happy or too comfortable with that side of things and she would never ask me any questions about my private life yet in many respects she was surrounded by far more outgoing people in that field than me with movie directors and even close friends like Peter Lawford.

Rock told me that it was his studio Universal who balked at him starring with Marilyn in " Bus Stop " It was as ever money you know because Fox wanted to offer me the role but Universal whom I was signed to demanded along with my agent a bigger slice of the fee and so yes it was a great shame as I think it would have been wonderful to co-star with her in many respects, Rock went on " It's hard now to imagine how the studio controlled a star back then you know" The studio system was a big part of the success of your career . It was a system that made sure that the biggest studios in Hollywood were in total control of the movies they made and that the movies would be distributed. The biggest studios at that time were divided into two groups. 'MGM, Paramount, Warner Bros., RKO and Fox and 'The Little Three': Universal, Colombia and United Artists. So you never really had a say but I spoke with Marilyn afterwards about this and she adored working with Don Murray in the movie so it all worked well in the end.

Rock also admitted that Marilyn herself confided some untruths about her life and how she her entire persona and bio was manufactured by the studio. She was never really an orphan. Fox designed the "vulnerable" past lies so women wouldn't hate her. It mostly worked but when I say she was not an orphan she was in some sense but they ramped up the quota to make it look worse and she was happy to go along with it. We all did I mean we were told whom to date and what to eat where to go and so forth so yeah while Marilyn may have seemed pushed around she did agree to a lot too to get on ...

Rock looked great and was very relaxed when I asked him a ton of questions but what really shocked me was his openness about him and other stars. It was hard to remember that even then a big star talking about his sexual exploits was rather shocking and one of such iconic status as Rock Hudson but he spoke openly about James Dean, Tab Hunter, Tony Curtis and many more he laughed when he spoke of how the bosses of Universal would get him to show the new signing around the lot which of course I could then work out who my next rival was going to be "he laughed.

Rock admitted that he owed lots of his career to Lew Wasserman but he was a tough guy you know who kept people on a leash really and Universal was a cheap studio we all knew that but we all hoped that we could get a loan out to work at one of the better studios and so that is how I ended up yet again been considered "Let's Make Love" with Marilyn.

Let's Make Love was a 1960 musical comedy film made by 20th Century Fox and It was directed by George Cukor and produced by Jerry Wald from a screenplay by Norman Krasna, Hal Kanter, and Arthur Miller. It starred Marilyn Monroe, Yves Montand, and Tony Randall. It would be Marilyn's s last musical film performance.

Rock told me "she wanted me to be the leading man in the movie but then my agent got wind that many had turned it down including my good pal Paul Newman, Gregory Peck and many others but Marilyn was not the problem again really. The movie was a dud and Fox wanted her working after the success of " Some Like It Hot " while she was still hot and of course the other stars were not keen on Arthur Miller's involvement in the movie as he was seen as dull and a little too highbrow and the last I heard was that they had signed up the French actor Yves Montand, , Rock added " I know that Marilyn was not happy about this because he spoke very little English but like her she said " Well at least he is good looking " so that was how that deal fell through.

Rock was rather said when he spoke of the final time he worked with Marilyn which was just months before her death at the 1962 Golden Globes awards of which he was a presenter "She looked better than ever I mean truly stunning but mentally she was not in great shape. She won an award on the night and as I am sure you know she was very drunk when she arrived at the awards and proceeded to get worse really I mean it was a tragic sense of this is happening and we can't help, Rock recalled that Marilyn spent a while chatting with Judy Garland and they were both hugging and crying at one point but I know her date who was a young man she had met in Mexico *was not happy about been left alone so again she managed to pick someone who was totally wrong for her really".*

Rock states that he received a call from Fox direct about appearing in the movie "Something Got to Give "as Marilyn had put his name down on a list of people that she would like to co-star with in the movie and hence the call direct because has Rock pointed out "Fox at this time were running on empty money wise thanks to Cleopatra and everyone in the town knew this".

Rock stated his reason for not wanting to do the movie was not really about the money "although it was bad "he told me but simply because he had done this type of movie over and over with Doris Day and "I wanted to make sure I could get a career going and show people I could act not just act the fool and be handsome on the screen which is what the role was".

Rock assured me that the role was that of Dean Martin's in the end because "they were offering it to lots of people and all turned it down because they knew that a Monroe shoot could last a long time and so when she heard this Marilyn called Rock direct.

"She was not happy about this at all but we both agreed that the script was not funny and even she could not save it "Rock was rather honest about the next question when he said "she had a terrible time agreeing to play a mother for the first time on screen. Not just for her acting but vanity really as she felt people would feel she was old and not a sex symbol anymore so she had a certain amount of self-awareness really when it came to her and her career for sure, Rock

admits that they did not part on the best terms although he told me he did see her again in the Hilton Beverley Hills not long before she passed away " she was sitting alone, no makeup she looked tired and had been fired by Fox by then and I wanted to go over and say hello and so all the stuff you should do but as I say with Marilyn there were boundaries really and often or not she could ignore if out ... I know it sounds crazy but she was like that you know. Off the wall as you may say".

As we concluded Rock seemed fascinated why she and more so I was still so interested in her as a relevant star today. "She would have loved all this really I mean she would not have expected it because we never see ourselves as others do but I am sure she would have loved to think people still were keen on to know all about her".

I asked Rock who or what he thought was responsible for Marilyn's death and he was very open about this "To me Hollywood loves a mystery and there have been none bigger than this but I would also say that many people who were with her at that time must know more. I never liked her Dr or her housekeeper because you just got the feeling they were not really been honest but other than that I can't say no more because as with so many things unless you were there at that time we may never know the truth".

Rock Hudson was a huge star and little did I know that he was ill himself at this point I am sure he would not have told me anyway. But what I do remember is seeing how his once most handsome face was ravaged by the terrible illness of Aids and how the media treated him because of his role with Dynasty with Linda Evans, if you recall he had kissed her on screen and there was this big storm over if / how / when she may too have picked up the disease which was terrible to see having admired the actor for such a long time

Despite going to great lengths to hide his secret, Rock's fall at the Ritz in France ultimately tipped off the world that the actor was suffering from a raging illness. President Reagan called to check up on the actor after it was learned Hudson had been rushed to a hospital following his sudden collapse in France, where he had gone for undercover treatments of the antiviral HPA-23, then unavailable in the United States, His good friend Elizabeth Taylor called Hudson every night during his stay at a hospital in France, immediately after his fall,

Rock Hudson died on 2 October 1985, I shall be forever grateful for his kindness and his compassion in telling me some of his glorious Hollywood stories.

Lauren Bacall

I have met the great Lauren Bacall on a few occasions but like all of Marilyn's associates you get the feeling that in her case she was not happy having the interview deflected away from her and someone as she said " not in the present " Lauren took some warming up I recall as she was not happy to speak about the past due to the fact " I think it all goes so quickly so it better to live in the moment and when people ask me about what say Marilyn Monroe was like it's not like we were the best of friends or anything I mean we made a movie together which was very successful and all that but it was long time ago... ... ...

Lauren reached the peak of her popularity in 1953, when she co-starred with Betty Grable and Marilyn Monroe in the hugely successful screen comedy, how to Marry a Millionaire. It was as she stated "a well ahead of its time movie because essentially we were three dames on the make and yet I was seen has the hard-faced one of the trio yet this was not the case. It's how the filmed played though and I got a lot of work from it.

She got on well with Betty Grable, "she was a doll I mean a total professional and we hit it off straight away which I was glad about "However Monroe exasperated her almost beyond endurance. Lauren told me she regarded her as selfish, ill-mannered and unprofessional, "She really was not cut out to be an actress I mean she would never look at you or the director but the god damned drama coach who sat in the whole time. I said to the director why do we have Marilyn if the drama coach is better "Lauren also pointed out that Marilyn would go into a trance-like persona and only look at your forehead while filming as the coach had told her "you look more sexy yet she moaned about wanting to be taken seriously all the time. A complete paradox of a woman "Lauren did say that Betty was "very fond of her and went out of her way to make her welcome as she had essentially taken over her crown at Fox and Betty knew this but there was no malice about it all. That's why I liked her".

I got the feeling that Lauren was not a fan of Marilyn but not because she was envious of her on going fame but later on the interview she admitted "I think I was sort of stuck in a rut and she was at the peak of her powers. We all had it and I knew that mine was gone and you know it's something that never comes back at all".

Sir Laurence Olivier

Laurence Olivier was one of the most acclaimed actors of the 20th century, known for his numerous Shakespeare roles on stage and screen as well as memorable turns in more modern classics. Born in England in 1907, Laurence Olivier was one of the most acclaimed actors of the 20th century, known for his career-defining performances of Shakespearean roles on stage and screen, as well memorable turns in modern classics such as Wuthering Heights and Marathon Man. He was knighted by King George VI and later made Baron Olivier of Brighton by Queen Elizabeth II, who also gave him the Order of Merit. Outside of his acting career, Olivier is remembered for his love affair and tempestuous marriage to actress Vivien Leigh.

When I tell people how I actually met the great actor they are real stunned but this is truthfully how it happened. I was at the Queen's Hotel in Leeds which at that time also hosted the Jimmy Young TV programme for Yorkshire as well as various other shows. No idea why they did this but I presume they could get huge audiences in the ballroom area. So one day I went to ask about tickets and how I could attend the audience which Mum & Dad said I could do if I got tickets. After enquiring I walked over to the lounge area and you have to remember I am quite young at this stage and not totally sure how I should act or behave in such glamorous surroundings. Looking at the TV guide I looked up and in the corner sat all alone was none other than the greatest actor of our generation. Sir Laurence Oliver. He was of course wonderfully dressed yet older looking than I thought he would be. Reading a paper and had a walking cane at the side of his chair. A full glittering tea service was sat in front of him. Heart pounding as you can guess by now I went over to introduce myself. I became a fan of Larry as friends call him after his highly publicized autobiography which was in my local library and this is how I became aware of his involvement in the movie "The Prince and the showgirl "As I have stated before I was a book worm and these books fuelled my quest for all things Hollywood and the great movies that were made but meeting Sir Larry was at first…underwhelming.

"Good Afternoon May I "Larry looked up from his paper and looked bored "What do you want? he asked rather bluntly "Are you Sir Laurence Oliver. The great actor of our time". That got his attention he looked up smiled and said "Dear Boy what on earth are you talking about and how does someone so young even know who I am?"

I blurted out that I had read his book and thought it was brilliant and was fascinated that he had worked with one of my all-time movie favourites in Marilyn Monroe… "Oh no not another one "he replied and to which I asked "One what Sir?

Larry asked me to sit next to him on the long sofa and we began or rather he began to tell me all about his career and what a delight he was. He was in Leeds to film the great TV series "Brides head Revisited "at Castle Howard and told me all about the production and the book. This was at least a year before the dram was actually transmitted so a real exclusive really although way too young to do anything about it.

Larry told me he was waiting at the Queens hotel because the production company may have needed him to stay an extra day but he wished to get back to London and this was his stop over yet he was unaware if anyone actually at reception remembered him sitting there waiting for an important call. "Shall I go and check for you Sir, "Do call me Larry dear boy and yes that would be divine".

I went along to the reception desk and felt very important but to my glee there was no phone call so this meant that Sir Larry would be mine and trapped for a while, He sat back and I asked him if I could interview with my cassette recorder as I took it everywhere "Why and well yes if you must "so began a brilliant conversation that until now has never been revealed at all to anyone else.

"I think everyone loves Marilyn now you see because she has become a legend and those that were associated with her are supposed to say wonderful things about the deceased but for me I think the ordeal on "Prince "was terrible. She was though a beautiful delight but again my memory is of her mad drama teacher who kept well out of my way because she was a Freud I mean she hindered Marilyn so much because the girl had a natural talent which even now looking at the movie is glorious but she needed constant assurance at all levels all the time which was somewhat

draining, Larry was honest if nothing else when he said " I loathed her at the time dear boy which you may find shocking but again she had the cast in tears and worn out one even took to drink but she floated past it all in a trance to be frank, I do think though that my ego was bruised I mean she was the hottest thing and remained so yet she never really warmed to me yet she actually booked me to be in her film which I always found confusing...was my ego hurt. You bet for sure" he laughed.

Larry was grumpy and frank but unlike so many stars who have met the great lady he was honest and of course possibly endured more than most while working on a film with her. His final words were haunting though "I do find it amazing that even after all these years her image lives on and that has to be something no one can manufacture so whatever she had she had something special and yes I was part of her story so for that I am grateful truly I am "

Frank Sinatra Jr

Frank Sinatra Jr went for the almost impossible goal of matching his father's famous voice, for a while his timbre was similar to the late singer's baritone, but that was just it he was not his father and as he explained to me "How do you live up to that?"

Sinatra Jr did not that badly at all when you consider he released several albums and playing some major venues, including Ronnie Scott's in 2012 which is where I encountered him, but he never found stardom. "In the entertainment business", he said, "the mark of success is your name coupled with a famous motion picture, television series or hit record. I have had none of those things. Therefore, I do not regard what I do as a success but he admitted to me that his stint on the hit cartoon comedy "Family Guy "has done far more for me than many other adventures I have undertaken.

Grumpy and not at all friendly despite his demand for full approval of any interview he soon warmed when I genuinely explained that I did enjoy his show (I did) and only wanted to show him in a positive light he told me bluntly 'When I gave the eulogy at my father's funeral in 1998 I said he had the magnetic appeal of a Valentino, the attraction of a James Dean, the sex appeal of a Marilyn Monroe and the undying adulation given to an Elvis Presley. Frank added "I did that as he never stopped loving Marilyn Monroe he adored her like so many men but again he could not save her alone. Did I meet her sure? Frank Jr was warming up a bit now and explained "she was a bright lady nothing like you would think but also she was complicated. By that I mean she morphed into whatever she thought you wanted her to be because she had no ground or base of her own. Do you understand?

He went on "I saw her many times with my father and then again with others. She was totally different as a person because she played whoever she thought she was that day and you know that is clever but also dangerous really simply because she then went home and I guess had no idea what or who she was then?

Frank Jr admitted "she was great to look at but also could be unrecognizable because it took a long time to "create "that look and of course be camera ready but I would say naturally she was one of the most beautiful women ever. It was also her grace she, moved swiftly and sat with the grace and manners of a titled lady but I also saw the ugly side of her been drugged up and drunk which was hard to take…

Frank Jr told me he thinks the reason why stars like Marilyn and his father remain so high profile even today is simple "sheer talent they both had it and it comes along once in a blue moon but again people will take to their hearts who they love and like many people I do have a soft spot for Marilyn Monroe she was really something else.

Andy Williams

Andy Williams, born on December 3, 1927, in Wall Lake, Iowa, made his singing debut at age 8 as part of the Williams Brothers quartet. He started a solo career in 1952 and had several hit singles, including his rendition of "Moon River" from the film Breakfast at Tiffany's. He launched The Andy Williams Show on NBC in 1962 and opened The Andy Williams Moon River Theatre in Branson, Missouri, in 1992. He died on September 25, 2012,

On Marilyn Monroe Andy simply told me " she was breathtakingly beautiful - admirers abound spoke of words like 'ethereal' and 'exquisite and they were right she was well a true on off and she had no idea that was the best bit, Andy was relaxing in his hotel suite ahead of one of his final ever shows and visits to London where he told me " I was booked to appear at the Frank Sinatra Lodge in Las Vegas and she was a guest many times but while she knew she was beautiful she had no idea in many respects that she was also talented.

He added "I think she was used by many around her but also she hooked up with the strangest people I think looking back because they in her mind could not use her yet others did like co-stars and agents etc. I know she was used by the drama coach because they tried to get me to sign up using her name I mean did she know about this really? I would think not.

Andy has his own thoughts on Marilyn's association with the Kennedy clan as he was also great mates with Robert and his wife but he recalls the fateful day when Bobby was shot.

I was at the Ambassador Hotel in LA, in my dressing in his room and watching Kennedy — who was in the lobby downstairs — on TV talking to reporters, when a man stepped out of the crowd and shot Kennedy three times. I just stood still he recalled, who had heard the shots on his television, then he rushed to the hospital where his friend lay on a bed, soaked in blood. Friends brought fresh clothes to dress the body, but had forgotten a tie. Williams took off his own and offered it to Bobby's widow, Ethel and told her 'I was putting that on when I heard the shots, ' At the funeral in New York, Williams sang The Battle Hymn of the Republic, and as his voice was broadcast outside St Patrick's Cathedral, thousands of mourners lining the streets joined in.

Andy told me "I think she was madly in love with him towards the end and like many people rejection is hard to take when your Marilyn Monroe whatever you think I believe that in her mind she felt that he should you know have treated her better "Did I think they were lovers? I asked him "Well it's an interesting question because it's not something anyone will know until we meet the Lord is it, I think people like to think they may have been to be spurned and all that but truthfully I have no idea. I could tell she liked him but then she did that with every guy she met. Made them feel like a millionaire so how could I truly know; I will tell you this though. After she died he never spoke of her much again which knowing him told me he was very upset over it all. It was never really a discussion again even if people brought it up so again who knows ...

Richard Wattis

Richard Wattis was an invaluable asset to any UK comedy film or TV programme for nearly thirty years. Much associated with the Eric Sykes TV series for the latter part of his career. He was often seen in officious roles, such as snooty shop managers, secretaries and policemen. I met him very briefly while at the BBC as a child and he was appearing in the hit children's show "Jackanory "he was kind, funny and talked to any child as an adult but his language was fruity and very direct. Of Marilyn he told my audio tape "I liked her to begin with I mean she was this huge Hollywood star but then that is the problem you see. She was a huge star and had no regard for us mere mortals standing around waiting for her to appear... "Richard breaks off at this point but quickly concludes "I think looking back it was all way too much for her really I mean she was great and superb in the role but being in England and producing the movie too must have taken its toll. He did add "She tried to be nice to me but if I am honest and frank I was not very nice to her young man and yes I do regret it".

With that Richard went off and I was in total awe of him simply because he starred in one of my favourite shows "Sykes "on TV at that time and to have met him was great but again it's interesting to see just what he thought of her after all these years.

Richard Burton

My encounter with the world-famous actor took place in 1981 at the world famous Dorchester Hotel in London his former wife Elizabeth Taylor had made her stage debut in Little Foxes at the Victoria Palace Theatre and I was basically hanging around the hotel foyer in the hope of simply meeting him simple as that but again I was lucky because he simply strode in and I strode up to him and simply said " I am trying to be reporter and think that if I get an interview with a huge star like you I could be one " Richard Burton turned to me directly and looked me in the eye and said " Well let's see if we can't get you a job " He directed me to the hotel lounge where he offered me tea and himself coffee which amazed me as I thought he might just have drunk all the time ...

The story is this while he talked about his career he told me how he was almost in a Marilyn Monroe film which was of course "the Prince and the showgirl "I liked the look of it all and I knew that Larry liked me but again I was not chosen. Truthfully I thought she was a superb thing and wanted to get to know her. I was you might say a Marilyn fan".

Burton was a kind soul and knew what he was telling me. He looked ill and grey but was charming itself and really knew how to make a story work. Richard added "I did meet her on a few occasions and she was so highly intelligent but my wife .... Well she was not that much of a fan really I suppose you could say they were rivals but I am not quite sure how that was worked out Richard also told me that he was offered a cameo by Zancuk for the 1960 Marilyn film " Let's Make Love " but again I spurned it simply because I felt it was just a cameo but when I then saw the list of cameo's I was annoyed with myself " Burton like many added " We saw her quite a few times in Hollywood but she was never glammed up you know she looked like a beautiful doll but not in Marilyn mode she knew when to draw that one out but truthfully I can say I was thrilled to know her simply because she had such an enduring quality about her and one can only hope for some of the same ".

Marlene Dietrich

Marlene Dietrich, was a magnetic movie star and singer who was an international symbol of glamour and sex for more than half a century Marlene was an accomplished violinist prior to an injury to one of her hands. She decided to pursue an acting career and auditioned at the Berlin school of drama, supporting herself by working in a glove factory.

*As you can imagine I had a tough time at school after all I was
constantly chasing around and nagging my parents to go along and
meet / see / touch my favourite stars. But back then huge stars did
come to town this is where I met the great Dietrich first at her
London hotel and then when she invited back stage at that
Wimbledon theatre where she was appearing. I recall asking my dad
why she was stuck out so far away from the West End after all she
was a huge star his reply "It's a booking and acts are always
grateful".*

*Listening again to the recording Marlene was kind generous and in
a way fascinated by someone so young that could be interested in
her career and yet knew so much. We naturally got around to
Marilyn and she says this "She called me a lot on the phone as she
was very lonely it was a shame because she was quite shy in fact this
was a factor for her plus she was a sex symbol and she often spoke
about age and time running out which is utter madness you know".*

*Marlene said that even when she met Marilyn first in the mid-50s she
was worried about her career all the time " That is how we became
friends because she liked to talk in the night you know when she was
alone but I think again it was a failure on her part really because
she was so talented and had so much to offer " Marlene recalled " I
remember telling her how much I enjoyed her performance in " Sone
Like it Hot " after all I had worked also with Billy Wilder and he
could be annoying she giggled ... Marilyn told me "You did, All I
can see is a fat pig up there on screen so it's not easy for me to
watch".*

Marlene poured some tea and added "You see that is all she saw. We saw a great comedy performance and she was super in the role but for Marilyn everything was based on looks and that really was the problem, Marlene also told me that Marilyn was keen to get her opinion on the planned remake of Marlene's most famous film "The Blue Angel "which would have seen Marilyn take on the role of Lola.

Marlene reveals "she was nervous about it because again she thought she was too old but I told her I thought the idea was a bad one again simply because I don't like remakes and despite what people think it never really works again the second time around so I think she did take this on board because it was never discussed again with me and I know she liked my opinions as I did her".

Marlene concluded that she was not shocked that Marilyn had died so young "she had a terrible last few years and for me I always thought it's amazing she was able to function but I know she was addicted to tablets and this can only lead to bad things. I did miss her a lot as does the world.

Tony Curtis

Tony Curtis, the Bronx tailor's son who became a 1950s movie heartthrob and then a respected actor with such films as "Sweet Smell of Success, " "The Defiant Ones" and "Some Like It Hot, Curtis moved to more substantial roles, starting in 1957 in the harrowing show business tale "Sweet Smell of Success. In 1958, "The Defiant Ones" brought him an Academy Award nomination as best actor for his portrayal of a white racist escaped convict handcuffed to a black escapee, Sidney Poitier. The following year, he donned women's clothing and sparred with Marilyn Monroe in one of the most acclaimed film comedies ever, Billy Wilder's "Some Like It Hot". Curtis also found his own princess: in 1951 he married actress Janet Leigh, she of Hitchcock fame. (They had two actress daughters, Jamie Lee and Kelly, and divorced in 1962.)

I was lucky enough to call Tony a friend after many interviews. I had met him many times on red carpets here in England and at the

Oscars. Always charming always good fun and never shy about spilling the beans. We became friends so that when he came to London he would root me out to chat, sometimes in his hotel lounge or we filmed interviews which led me to have many interviews with him that have never been screened...Tony of course was a huge star and loved being a star he truly loved the fans coming up and asking for autographs and pictures. I never saw him refuse anyone a scribe.

Tony told me that when he landed the studio contract with Universal he already knew Marilyn quite well "she was and remained a lady but she also used people you know she treated any guy like a god more so if she felt they could be useful but I never resented her for that because she had this light about her and she was not cruel in any way she just had no real upbringing so she did what she thought was right and well that upset many people really.

Tony told me that while both were trying their luck at breaking into the big time they would often meet up and talk about new signings. Tony added "I was signed up with Tab Hunter and Rock Hudson and basically they played us off you know. You had to keep fit, look good and all that because there was always another pretty guy waiting in line but the thing I recall is that Marilyn had zero ideas that Rock was gay. Not many did but even when she knew that he did not have a girlfriend or anything she had romantic illusions about him simply because she could not understand that not all men would not find her attractive. When I told her he was gay she accused me of lying so that she would just be my girl but that what was she liked really nice but oblivious to the truth.

Tony did make a confessional bombshell to me though one interview when she told me how he became good pals with Rock and a lot of his gay pals "It never bothered me because I knew quite a few were hitting on me and yes I had my moments I can say that now right? But sure Rock hit on me all the time and while I liked women I was flattered when guys told me I was good looking but that was it like Marilyn I was insecure".

I pushed Tony again "So were you and Rock an item "Tony laughed and told me "I had my moments for sure and we became good friends but I know that Rock wanted more and even thought we could settle down but it was not for me and you know who knew how all this would pan out but I was not the only big star that Rock enjoyed fun with you know. Don't think I am unique.

Tony told me many times about the "Some Like It Hot "stories with Marilyn and all the late stuff but he did give an insight into why he felt she had problems "The Strasberg's were such users you know I mean Paula mad as a witch. Failed actress herself yet telling Marilyn how to act I mean I did bring it up with her many times but it was like she was blind to them or simply felt she needed them. Even the husband Arthur (Miller) seemed to be brained washed into thinking they had something to offer which they did not at all "Marilyn like me never got an Oscar or was even close "You know something, " says Curtis, who is suddenly pulling me in closer, "I became a really good actor". He complains that the film industry never appreciated him and failed to give him an Oscar, preferring the "method-acting bulls**t". I think that is why I resented what the Strasbergs did to a lot of actors and yet I know for a fact she loathed *them too at times but felt trapped. She gave them huge amounts of money and they would bill her all the time with their "work "what sort of friend is that though I ask you.*

Curtis parodied the voice of his idol and friend Cary Grant in "Some Like It Hot ", while pretending to be an eligible millionaire. It was a brilliant piece of acting. "I was really proud of that, " but Marilyn hated the idea as "she had worked with Carey in "Monkey Business "years ago and felt that he would not be happy with it but thankfully Billy Wilder loved the idea and that was that but I found out later that it came from Arthur Miller. He was a total bore you know, Tony admitted "Half the problems in the movie were created by Miller and the other half by the Strasberg's so I know that without them she would have been far better.

Tony though holds out on his friend dying as suicide as odd "I truly believe that people around her like the housekeeper who ends up as a spy for her obsessed Doctor and even the PR lady Pat Newcombe she must have known more. While I liked the Kennedy's I would not have got that close and yet this lady who is the self-proclaimed "Best Friend "of Marilyn ends up working for the Kennedy's after her death...suspicious you bet I am but again nothing was investigated".

Tony told me that he felt people assumed that he and Marilyn were not friends after that "Hitler" comment but it's not the case "she and I did speak at various events. Yes, I was stupid and yes I should never have quipped that but again it was that mad bitch Paula Strasberg who rushed along and told her I mean why would you do that. Because that was her worth to Marilyn not as an acting coach but as a gossip and feeding her ego which was fine I might add.

Some Like It Hot was an instant success, and Marilyn won a Golden Globe for her role. It remains her most popular movie, and is now considered one of the greatest comedies ever made. Tony Curtis is justly proud of the film, and of his own fine performance as he told me < I know people are fascinated by my association with Marilyn and naturally I do get it but to me she was just a girl who made bad choices. Talented oh yes and beautiful too very stunning even more so without all the makeup but I am not sure if she had not died so young if it would have continued as age was a huge problem for her".

Tony added "she worried about looking old on screen and hated the way she looked in the movie but she was pregnant and of course she drank quite a bit but I think well she told me it was easier for men like me who were good looking and fit simply because we age and can get grace where as women just get wrinkles... 'Tony also reiterated "Marilyn was a loner. That is why she was so many hours on the phone. She would call people during the night. Me anyone and juts wanted to talk yet she was not one to sit and hound you for company"'

As Tony pointed out "when we are on the set of 'Hot' she always had her breaks in the dressing room or simply alone not because she was been rude or anything like that but she assumed that she would not be wanted that was the level of insecurity she had yet she was the star of the picture" Tony told me that he met Marilyn last in the last year of her life while at a Sinatra function and he was not pleased to see how ill she looked "I think she had an eating disorder because she had shed so much weight and looked well ill ... I did mention this but she told me that the studio was more than happy with her weight loss and she liked it too".

After a while I noticed her sat alone in the corner and in a world of her own really. I know she was using drugs a lot but I think at this point no one was also saying no to her and while I think her death was strange because she had so much to live for and was back on top I do think that her ill-gotten friends were partly to blame for the mess she ended up in. Do I think I could have saved her? I know having a child would have saved her as she was great with my children and anyone's on the set in the fact that is when she came alive as she knew children wanted nothing from her except her.

As Tony prepared to say goodbye for the last time our final meeting was at the famous restaurant in Harrods. Just me him and a cameraman he was lovely and as he wheeled himself away now in his chair I was feeling choked as I knew that this could be the last time I would see him...he turned around in his chair and said "Bye Neil and thanks truly for your friendship.

Celeste Holm

Oscar-winning actress Celeste Holm was a star of the Broadway stage and movies, Holm won the best-supporting actress Academy Award for "Gentleman's Agreement" in 1947. She was nominated for the same honour in 1949 for "Come to the Stable" and 1950 for "All

about Eve, " according to the Academy database Fox briefly
suspended her in 1950 "for refusing other roles she felt were
beneath her". But she was brought back that same year to play the
role of Karen Richards in "All About Eve". She was again
nominated for the best supporting actress Oscar. She shocked
Hollywood by buying out her Fox contract after "All About Eve" to
return to Broadway, despite her rising big screen stardom. Once
back in New York, Holm also began a long career acting in
television.

Ms Holm was charm itself when I met her backstage in London and
was refreshingly honest about her one time co-star Marilyn Monroe,
giggly, fun and yes a total star she was very direct about her one
time famous co-star telling me " she is the one even today people ask
me about all the time its Marilyn yet I suspect that people think I
should be mean about her as she was terrible on set with her time
keeping but years later you can now see what she left behind and we
were very lucky to be part of her world however short it was.

She recalls Marilyn Monroe, who was just starting out in pictures
when she made All About Eve was very insecure working among
such great established talent and struggled to hold her own. Bette
Davis and some of the other actors could get impatient with her
inexperience, but Monroe worked hard and tried to put forth her best
efforts. I have to admit that I was jealous of her and yet in awe at the
same time because she made it all so convincing this little girl lost
act with the women's body but you don't get on without some steel
and she had plenty about her because her man at that time was a
huge agent called Johnny Hyde. Celeste continued "She did not care

*for him I know that but what she did was drag him along knowing
that this was the key to her moment you know and yes I truly
admired her for it, she was a genius really because she was playing
a role daily within herself and that is a very complex mind very
clever indeed.*

*Filming the hit movie "All About Eve "was trying for Marilyn as she
was up against some strong talents like Bette and Anne but as
Celeste recalls she had someone on her side "I know for a fact that
Johnny Hyde had a quiet word with Bette as if to warn her off as she
was great friends with Zanuck who in turn was keen to work out
what Johnny had found in terms of a new star. Zanuck though was
not that impressed and I recall one day him been on the set when we
were shooting and Marilyn blew a scene ten times yet they were
simple lines…It was Bette who helped calm her down and helped her
through the scene even though it was Bette's scene which we all
secretly found amusing really.*

*It appears according to Celeste that Marilyn was "alone, aloof and
very unfriendly unless you were useful, I am not being unkind at all
when I say this as the myth takes over and people start saying nice
things about the deceased but I liked her I really did but she was
beyond clever yet in the end it all got caught up with her. She added
"I saw her in Hollywood not long before she died and it was all
them on her face. The heartache and broken dreams we spoke but
she was very untrusting about all kinds of things and I think by this
time with the failed marriages and career burning out she looked
like someone who wanted a friend but never really had one and yet
she rejected kindness directly out of hand. I was very sad when I*

heard she had passed away as she was way too young and so much more talent to come to the surface but she got wrapped up in the wrong things and people so for her it was not a happy ending".

In 1950, Marilyn moved into her own apartment while she was being escorted by a new father-figure, the venerable Hollywood agent Johnny Hyde. When Hyde died from a heart attack in December 1950 Marilyn fell apart but as Celeste recalls "She was once again totally alone and no one fighting her corner which must have been hard to take yet again more rejection, she added "I do think at least that she credited him with creating her as an actress and he did more for her than anyone else and she knew it but sadly never lived to see what he had created. Who knows maybe that was a good thing given she ended life so early ....

Ethel Merman

Ethel Merman is best known as a gutsy, powerful musical comedy performer and remembered for her brassy style and powerful mezzo-soprano voice. Her 14 movies included "Alexander's Ragtime Band", "There's No Business Like Show Business" and "It's a Mad, Mad, Mad, Mad World".

Meeting the great Ms Merman was terrifying in all the possible ways simply because she was a tough New York broad who I was told would not be talking about her one-time co-star Marilyn Monroe as she was "bored rigid with the topic "But as ever charm and an easy going nature can get you a long way and Ethel as I was told to call her was a true Dame. A complete laugh who loved the fact she had a fan with her album "Ethel Merman Does Disco "I can't believe anyone bought it but I am flattered that you did "she bellowed in her dressing room at a London Theatre.

Ethel Merman performed with Marilyn in the 1954 movie musical "There's No Business Like Show Business, " along with such seasoned musical comedy veterans as Dan Dailey and Donald O'Connor. Monroe was still basking in the glow of her sexy "Diamonds Are a Girl's Best Friend" number from the film "Gentlemen Prefer Blondes".

The cast had years of experience on the stage. Monroe didn't. "Ethel would say 'All right, where's the blond?' Marilyn was always late on the set if she had to work with me because I think I scared the you-know-what out of her, " Ethel said. But at the end of the movie and this is never reported she gave me a present and thanked me for been a task master and getting a performance out of her so yes I do think the story about me and Marilyn needed addressing.

"I never saw anybody work so hard, " noted Merman "She did such a good job and personally, I think she stole the whole damn show. I just think she was thrown into a nest of vipers". And the studio wanted us not to get on because in the 50's you had all these scandal magazines popping up who needed feeding on a daily basis. It was not Marilyn's fault at all that she could not hit marks and stuff like that I mean she was a sex symbol for goodness sake and yet we were all seasoned pros to a degree.

Ethel though admitted she was none too keen on many of the stars in the film "I know that Fox wanted Marilyn in it as she was their biggest star plus they paid her a very low salary they were truly mean to her yet she really had no one on her side at all looking after those things. I often loaned her money. Nothing huge but it got to that I mean she was dressed by the studio in stunning gowns and looked amazing yet the poor girl had nothing in to eat at home". Ethel admitted that "She was a very good and experienced film actress, but she could forget so many of the mechanical techniques. She would constantly miss her marks so she would be out of focus or out of the light or in a shadow. I think it was a lack of confidence which we all found amazing really because I had no experience of that and I told her so but she would look at me with eyes wide open and say "Oh but you have that voice I mean that is a talent what do I have "she left you bewildered at times. She went on "the camera loved, she was still terrified of going before the camera and broke out in a rash all over her body. And would start to shake. I remember asking her if all this was in fact worth it you know I mean why put yourself through it but she just smiled and said it was her dream".

Ethel laughed when she recalled that Marilyn was shocked to discover that singer Johnny Ray was in fact homosexual "Are you sure? "she asked me, I asked her why "Well he looks at me like a man looks at a woman you know? "I tried to tell her that while she may like him he was far more interested in Dan Daily then her which she found very upsetting. Her ego was that fragile so in order to make sure we got through the movie it was an open secret that I made sure Johnnie flirted with her and that she had her own personal victory over me. "I adored her for it though because I am sure deep down she must have known. Everyone else did.

Martin Landau

Oscar-winning actor Martin Landau was a great interview and I met him quite a few times over the years at events, premieres and firstly while he played another Hollywood icon in the form of Bella Lugosi from the movie "Ed Wood".

Martin dated Marilyn briefly prior to her marriage to Arthur Miller and he told me that while she was the ultimate she was very complicated and I mean that in a kind way simply because she was an artist and wanted to be a great one you know she loved acting and wanted to learn so much she was like a sponge in that respect and far ahead of her time for sure, I met Marilyn when she came to New York to study with Lee Strasberg (former Actors Studio artistic director), I was at the Actors Studio. She was in Lee's private classes, and was also coming to the Studio. She saw me act, and wanted to do a scene with me, I was very flattered and she was this huge movie star taking a back seat from fame. Lee thought it a good idea because he felt if she asked for me then it would make doing the scene easier and he was right. We totally trusted each other as actors and got on well often going for coffee and sandwiches after class "Martin though has his own theory on that period of her life "I think that this was her college you know the student thing because while most there were struggling actors and had very little money she was living in this rather splendid apartment in the classy area of

• • •
144

New York but playing a role of a student with the classes so that is what I mean when I say she as complicated "

Martin told me that he believed that she went to the actor's studio not because Fox treated her badly but "She was there because she was dissatisfied. People perceived her as a Hollywood blonde bimbo. She was very needy and would go from being on top of her game to absolutely bereft of any self-belief or confidence and I mean zero in many respects which was hard to fathom because it was that dark basically. She seesawed between those two personalities quite a lot of times but again it could have been the pills as I know she had terrible times sleeping which made her edgy".

He recalls that When they went to the theatre she'd change her outfits many times. "We'd never see the first act of the play she was late for everything because she got hooked up into what people would say about what she was wearing to simply getting anywhere on time "He added "She was terrific .... I mean she made you feel like the luckiest guy in the world looking back she had that power but I don't do kiss and tells it's not my style I don't talk about those things, " he says, quietly.

Martin admitted that "I had a relationship with her. It was just before Arthur (Miller, the playwright whom she married in 1956). It was an interesting and unique in that relationship; I look at it very differently than the way I did then. She was incredibly attractive but very difficult. And you can't with that for long That's why I didn't". *It lasted? "Several months. But she had split personality and it was very tough never knowing "which one would show up in the middle of something". After the relationship ended, Martin and Monroe saw each other "a couple of times in passing" in New York and Los Angeles. She was incredibly attractive and fun to be with much of the time. When she wasn't she wasn't. I mean, that was the problem. She could get very withdrawn".*

Martin recalls he was at an airport in Rome changing planes in Rome in 1962 when he read that Monroe had died. "I was heartbroken. As the mystery unfolded I was more and more shocked. It didn't seem possible that she killed herself intentionally. It was possible she took more barbiturates than necessary, just losing count, or possibly it was foul play. Nobody knows and yet I do think she would find it amusing that even today people are still speaking about her and her career. I don't think she felt apart from her fans that anyone truly cared which was all very upsetting when you think about it.

James Garner

James Garner, the actor and producer, made his reputation in the late 1950s as the shrewd, anti-heroic gambler Bret Maverick in the Western series of the same name — and sealed it as the 1970s private investigator Jim Rockford in The Rockford Files. An ideal leading man, equally at home opposite Doris Day in romantic screen comedies such as Move Over Darling or in action blockbusters such as The Great Escape.

James Garner was almost one of Marilyn Monroe's last co-stars on the ill-fated movie "Somethings Got to Give "he told me the story of how and why he never happened.

James is best-known to Marilyn fans as Doris Day's leading man in Move Over Darling, the 1963 remake of Marilyn's unfinished last film, Something's Got to Give. However, Garner was originally chosen to star alongside Monroe in the movie but Fox reeling from overspending on the movie "Cleopatra "decided that they could get James cheaply but as he told me "My agent demanded $200, 000 to do the picture, but Fox thought I was a $150, 000-a-picture actor and would pay him no more. So I quit, but he added "I was also on a weekly TV show filming on the Fox lot and had heard that Marilyn was never on time and this could run over time so I did not want to lose the regular pay check of a weekly TV series for a movie that did not even have a script at this stage Then, only in Hollywood, the new producer, a man named Henry Weinstein, turned to Dean Martin that March, paying Martin double what Fox had wanted to pay me ".

James recalled though how he had a conversation with Marilyn on the phone about the role "she was warm kind, funny and desperate as "I really want you to star with me would you? She asked in that breathy voice of hers" James recalled that she seemed to be under the illusion that it was my fault and not Fox's as to why they would not pay me the money my agent requested me, I explained that I would love to co-star with her and that I was a huge fan of her work which seemed to please her but during the conversation she kept saying she thought the script was a dud and that it lacked any jokes

" I did say that she was not selling it to me but she added she felt with my presence and hers "we could make it work".

James recalls that he last saw her around the last time of her visits to the studios that summer of 1962 and she looked "very thin and drawn of course not on camera but in real life "and that her hair was pure white yet lifeless. "She was walking towards me when she realized that of course she had dropped me for Dean Martin so I teased her about it and then she asked me to forgive her. He added "I think I made a joke about her buying my lunch but she brought her own into the studio and offered to share with me her boiled eggs and chopped liver which stunk to high heaven so I declined. "

James though ever the gentleman admitted that he never felt this was a woman on the edge of a breakdown "Sure she looked sad but I know she hated the movie and then of course she had her own demons but no one really knows what happened to Marilyn in the final few weeks as she was a recluse in many ways and she was known privately as "Garbo "around the studio as you never really sway her out and about or at parties of functions she was a very private person really.

Made in the USA
Middletown, DE
15 December 2016